Lecture Notes in Computer Science 15423

The series Lecture Notes in Computer Science (LNCS), including its subseries Lecture Notes in Artificial Intelligence (LNAI) and Lecture Notes in Bioinformatics (LNBI), has established itself as a medium for the publication of new developments in computer science and information technology research, teaching, and education.

LNCS enjoys close cooperation with the computer science R & D community, the series counts many renowned academics among its volume editors and paper authors, and collaborates with prestigious societies. Its mission is to serve this international community by providing an invaluable service, mainly focused on the publication of conference and workshop proceedings and postproceedings. LNCS commenced publication in 1973.

Yang Wang · Liang-Jie Zhang
Editors

CLOUD Computing – CLOUD 2024

17th International Conference
Held as Part of the Services Conference Federation, SCF 2024
Bangkok, Thailand, November 16–19, 2024
Proceedings

 Springer

Editors
Yang Wang
Shenzhen Institute of Advanced Technology
Shenzhen, China

Liang-Jie Zhang 🆔
Shenzhen University
Shenzhen, China

ISSN 0302-9743   ISSN 1611-3349 (electronic)
Lecture Notes in Computer Science
ISBN 978-3-031-77152-1   ISBN 978-3-031-77153-8 (eBook)
https://doi.org/10.1007/978-3-031-77153-8

This Springer imprint is published by the registered company Springer Nature Switzerland AG
The registered company address is: Gewerbestrasse 11, 6330 Cham, Switzerland

If disposing of this product, please recycle the paper.

Preface

The 2024 International Conference on Cloud Computing (CLOUD 2024) aimed to provide an international forum to formally explore various business insights into all kinds of value-added "services". Cloud Computing is a key enabler in exploring business insights and economics of services.

CLOUD 2024 was a member of the Services Conference Federation (SCF). SCF 2024 had the following 10 collocated service-oriented sister conferences: 2024 International Conference on Services Computing (SCC 2024), 2024 International Conference on Big Data (BigData 2024), 2024 International Conference on AI and Multmodal Services (AIMS 2024), 2024 International Conference on Metaverse (Metaverse 2024), 2024 International Conference on Internet of Things (ICIOT 2024), 2024 International Conference on Cognitive Computing (ICCC 2024), 2024 International Conference on Edge Computing (EDGE 2024), 2024 International Conference on Blockchain (ICBC 2024), 2024 International Conference on Cloud Computing (CLOUD 2024), and 2024 International Conference on Web Services (ICWS 2024).

This volume presents the accepted papers of CLOUD 2024, held in Bangkok as an onsite conference during November 16–19, 2024. CLOUD 2024's major topics included but were not limited to: Infrastructure as a Service (IaaS), Platform as a Service (PaaS), Software as a Service (SaaS), Cloud Security and Privacy, Cloud Storage, Cloud Application Development, Cloud Performance Management, Industry-Specific Clouds, Business Models in Cloud, Serverless, 5G Cloud, Cloud Security, Privacy and Trust.

CLOUD 2024 received 16 submissions, and accepted 8 papers. Each was reviewed and selected by at least three independent members of the CLOUD 2024 International Program Committee in a single-blind review process. We are pleased to thank the authors whose submissions and participation made this conference possible. We also want to express our thanks to the Organizing Committee and Program Committee members for their dedication in helping to organize the conference and reviewing the submissions. We look forward to your great contributions as volunteers, authors, and conference participants in the fast-growing worldwide services innovations community.

November 2024   Yang Wang
                                                                   Liang-Jie Zhang

Organization

General Chair

Min Luo   Georgia Tech, USA

Program Chair

Yang Wang   Shenzhen Institute of Advanced Technology, China

Services Conference Federation (SCF 2024)

General Chairs

Ali Arsanjani   Google Cloud, USA
Wu Chou   Essenlix Corporation, USA

Coordinating Program Chair

Liang-Jie Zhang   Shenzhen University, China

CFO and International Affairs Chair

Min Luo   Georgia Tech, USA

Operation Committee

Jing Zeng   China Gridcom Co., Ltd., China
Yishuang Ning   Tsinghua University, China
Sheng He   Tsinghua University, China
Zhuolin Mei   Jiujiang University, China

Steering Committee

Calton Pu (Co-chair)	Georgia Tech, USA
Liang-Jie Zhang	Shenzhen University, China

CLOUD 2024 Program Committee

Roberto Di Pietro	Hamad Bin Khalifa University, Qatar
Sanjay Patel	Nirma University, India
Byungchul Tak	Kyungpook National University, South Korea
Yingwei Wang	University of Prince Edward Island, Canada
Yuehua Wang	Texas A & M University - Commerce, USA
Hailu Xu	California State University, USA
R. K. N. Sai Krishna	Yugabyte, USA
Rüdiger Schulze	IBM Germany Research & Development GmbH, Germany
Feng Chen	Louisiana State University, USA
Haopeng Chen	Shanghai Jiao Tong University, China
Jingshu Chen	Oakland University, USA
Shahram Ghandeharizadeh	USC, USA
Supratik Mukhopadhyay	Louisiana State University, USA
Jun Shen	University of Wollongong, Australia

Conference Sponsor – Services Society

The Services Society (S2) is a non-profit professional organization that has been created to promote worldwide research and technical collaboration in services innovations among academia and industrial professionals. Its members are volunteers from industry and academia with common interests. S2 is registered in the USA as a "501(c) organization", which means that it is an American tax-exempt nonprofit organization. S2 collaborates with other professional organizations to sponsor or co-sponsor conferences and to promote an effective services curriculum in colleges and universities. The S2 initiates and promotes a "Services University" program worldwide to bridge the gap between industrial needs and university instruction.

The Services Society has formed 5 Special Interest Groups (SIGs) to support technology and domain-specific professional activities.

- Special Interest Group on Services Computing (SIG-SC)
- Special Interest Group on Big Data (SIG-BD)
- Special Interest Group on Cloud Computing (SIG-CLOUD)
- Special Interest Group on Artificial Intelligence (SIG-AI)
- Special Interest Group on Metaverse (SIG-Metaverse)

About the Services Conference Federation (SCF)

As the founding member of the Services Conference Federation (SCF), the first **International Conference on Web Services (ICWS)** was held in June 2003 in Las Vegas, USA. Meanwhile, the First International Conference on Web Services - Europe 2003 (ICWS-Europe 2003) was held in Germany in October 2003. ICWS-Europe 2003 was an extended event of the 2003 International Conference on Web Services (ICWS 2003) in Europe. In 2004, ICWS-Europe was changed to the European Conference on Web Services (ECOWS), which was held in Erfurt, Germany. Sponsored by the Services Society and Springer, SCF 2018 and SCF 2019 were held successfully in Seattle and San Diego, USA. SCF 2020 and SCF 2021 were held successfully online and in Shenzhen, China. SCF 2023 was held successfully in Hawaii, USA. To celebrate its 21st birthday, SCF 2024 was held on November 16–19, 2024, in Bangkok, Thailand.

In the past 21 years, the ICWS community has been expanded from Web engineering innovations to scientific research for the whole services industry. The service delivery platforms have been expanded to mobile platforms, Internet of Things, cloud computing, and edge computing. The services ecosystem has gradually been enabled, value added, and intelligence embedded through enabling technologies such as big data, artificial intelligence, and cognitive computing. In the coming years, all transactions with multiple parties involved will be transformed to blockchain.

Based on technology trends and best practices in the field, the Services Conference Federation (SCF) will continue serving as the conference umbrella's code name for all services-related conferences. SCF 2024 defined the future of New ABCDE (AI, Blockchain, Cloud, BigData & IOT) and entered the AIGC for Services Era. The theme of SCF 2024 was **AI-Generated Services.** We are very proud to announce that SCF 2024's 10 co-located theme topic conferences were all centered around "services", while each focused on exploring different themes (web-based services, cloud-based services, Big Data-based services, services innovation lifecycle, AI-driven ubiquitous services, blockchain-driven trust service ecosystems, industry-specific services and applications, and emerging service-oriented technologies).

- Bigger Platform: The 10 collocated conferences (SCF 2024) were sponsored by the Services Society which is the world-leading not-for-profit organization (501(c)(3)) dedicated to the service of more than 30,000 worldwide Services Computing researchers and practitioners. A bigger platform means bigger opportunities for all volunteers, authors, and participants. Meanwhile, Springer provided sponsorship of the best paper awards and other professional activities. All the 10 conference proceedings of SCF 2024 will be published by Springer and indexed in the ISI Conference Proceedings Citation Index (included in Web of Science), Engineering Index EI (Compendex and Inspec databases), DBLP, Google Scholar, IO-Port, MathSciNet, Scopus, and ZBlMath.
- Brighter Future: While celebrating the 2024 version of ICWS, SCF 2024 highlighted the International Conference on AI and Multimodal Services (AIMS 2024) to build

the fundamental infrastructure for enabling AIGC services ecosystems. It will also lead our community members to create their own brighter future.

– Better Model: SCF 2024 will continue to leverage the invented Conference Blockchain Model (CBM) to innovate the organizing practices for all the 10 theme conferences. Senior researchers in the field are welcome to submit proposals to serve as CBM Ambassador for an individual conference to start better interactions during your leadership role in organizing future SCF conferences.

Contents

Fast and Accurate Query Scheme Over Encrypted Numerical Data in Cloud Environment

Yi Zhu[1]($\boxtimes$), Peigang Wang[1], Xuechun Hu[1], and Xiaolan Wang[2]

[1] School of Transportation and Information, Hubei Communications Technical College, Wuhan, China
zhuyi2250@163.com

[2] School of Maritime, Hubei Communications Technical College, Wuhan, China

Abstract. The query issue on outsourced encrypted data in cloud servers is a hot research topic in both the business and academic communities. Due to the high efficiency of Bloom filter in determining whether an element belongs to a set, the Bloom filter technique is often used as a fundamental component for constructing efficient query schemes. However, since Bloom filter may produce false positives with a certain probability, query schemes constructed based on Bloom filter may produce false positives in their query results with a certain probability. This paper combines prefix encoding, bilinear group operation and Bloom filter to construct a fast and accurate query scheme. Firstly, we construct a tree index, in which each node is associated with a range. We employ prefix encoding to process these ranges, then utilize Bloom filter to handle all the prefix codes of the ranges, and simultaneously employ bilinear group operation to process these prefix codes. The adoption of Bloom filter enables efficient data querying, while the adoption of bilinear group operation avoids the occurrence of false positive errors in the query results. Thus, our scheme can simultaneously support efficient and accurate query.

Keywords: Prefix Encode · Bloom Filter · Bilinear Group · Range Query · Cloud Environment

1 Introduction

In recent years, the rapid development of cloud computing has completely transformed various industries, revolutionizing the way of data management, data storage, data analyzing and processing [1]. With the top speed development of the technology an applications in cloud computing space, the support for the increasingly large data traffic and the break through resource limitations become a possibility, and it makes more intelligent and personalized services in daily life and production a reality. As a result, an increasing number of data owners including businesses and individuals, are opting to outsource their data to cloud servers. This strategic decision allows them to fully exploit the numerous advantages offered by cloud computing, including superb stability, improved reliability, enhanced scalability, accelerated deployment, and cost-effectiveness [2]. In the cloud-based model, a data user directly sends query requests to cloud server hosting the outsourced data. The cloud server executes the queries on the data and promptly deliver the query results back to the data user. This approach eliminates the important responsibility and heavy burdens of data management and maintenance for data owners, as well as the need for data users to interact with data owners for queries. By utilizing the elastic scalability, intelligent capabilities of managing and scheduling and computational power of cloud servers, efficient and dependable data query services are provided to data users. This shift to cloud-based data outsourcing has brought about changes in data management analyzing and processing methods especially in today's era of huge data demand. It enables data owners to focus on their core activities while leveraging the scalability and efficiency of cloud computing which it can totally support. Additionally, data users benefit from faster and more reliable query services, as the cloud servers offer robust computational resources and seamless access to the outsourced data.

However, there are many security risks associated with outsourced data in cloud servers [3, 4]. Internal personnel of the cloud server can access the stored data, while external attackers can monitor the query requests of data users and the query results returned by the cloud server, and even steal this outsourced data, posing a threat to the life and property security of both data owners and data users [5–8], causing huge economic losses and leading to serious consequences, with negative social impacts. Data encryption is one effective method to address the security issues of outsourced data in cloud servers. However, encrypted data is computationally indistinguishable therefore cannot support efficient queries. To enable efficient queries on encrypted data, researchers have proposed various methods for constructing secure indexes on the ciphertext of outsourced data. Among all the methods for constructing secure indexes, the one based on Bloom filters is widely adopted in this field, because it can be transformed into determining whether a data is within a query range. However, the secure index based on Bloom filters inherits a drawback of Bloom filters, which is the possibility of false positives in query results. Hence, the query results of the secure index based on Bloom filters may also contain false positives.

In order to efficiently query the ciphertexts of outsourced data in cloud servers and ensure that the query results do not have false positives, this paper employs prefix encoding to process the ranges, then utilizes a Bloom filter to handle the prefix codes of the ranges, and finally utilizes bilinear group operations to process the prefix codes of the ranges, ultimately achieving the effect of efficiently querying ciphertexts. The adoption of the Bloom filter enables efficient data querying, while the adoption of the bilinear group operations avoids the occurrence of false positive errors in the query results. Thus, our scheme can simultaneously support efficient and accurate query.

The contributions of this paper are as follows:

1. By employing prefix encoding, Bloom filters, and bilinear group operations, we have successfully built a secure index for numerical data ciphertexts. The design of this secure index enables efficient and secure querying of encrypted data, while also safeguarding the privacy and integrity of the data.
2. Building upon the secure index we constructed, we propose an efficient and accurate querying scheme for numerical data ciphertexts. This scheme not only allows for

fast retrieval and processing of encrypted data but also ensures the accuracy of query results, providing a convenient and reliable means of data access for data owners and users.

3. Through a series of experiments and security analyses, we have validated the efficiency, accuracy, and security of our scheme. Experimental results demonstrate that our scheme performs excellently under various conditions, showing significant advantages in handling large-scale datasets and protecting data privacy. Security analysis further confirms the reliability and resilience of our scheme against attacks, offering strong support for data security and privacy protection.

Through these contributions, we have presented an innovative and feasible solution for secure querying of encrypted numerical data, offering valuable insights and references for the advancement and practical application of data security in this field.

The structure of this paper is as follows. Section 2 presents related work. Section 3 provides background knowledge. Section 4 details the system model. Section 5 showcases the solution construction process. Section 6 conducts security analysis. Section 7 presents experimental results. Finally, Sect. 8 is the conclusion of this paper.

2 Related Work

Order-Preserving Encryption (OPE) methods are very special encryption techniques that allow data to maintain its order after encryption [9]. This means that the encrypted data can still be compared and sorted in the same order as the original data, without disrupting the ordering relationships between the data. OPE is commonly used in scenarios where encrypted data needs to be queried within a range or sorted, such as in database queries. Thus, OPE can be used to support efficient comparisons on the ciphertexts of numerical data. However, OPE also presents some security challenges. Because OPE requires maintaining the order relationships between data, attackers may be able to infer information about the original data by observing the encrypted data, potentially leading to information leakage.

The range query schemes based on public key encryption methods support range query over encrypted numeric data effectively. Compared to OPE methods, the range query method based on public key encryption has a significant advantage in that it does not expose the order relationship between plaintexts when conducting range queries. However, public key encryption systems require complex mathematical operations to perform encryption and decryption, leading to significant computational overhead and slowing down the data querying process. When scaled up to handle massive amounts of data, this inefficiency is further exacerbated as the computational demands increase exponentially with the growth of data volume, impacting the overall performance and responsiveness of the system [2].

Bucketization schemes divide all the data into multiple parts. In each data partition, all the data within it is treated as a unit which is called a bucket. Specifically, all the data in a bucket is encrypted and also searched as a unit [10]. Therefore, compared to OPE methods, bucketization schemes can effectively protect the ordering relationships between the data. When performing a range query, all the ciphertexts of the data in a bucket, which intersects with the queried range, are all returned as the search results. Due to the very small computational cost involved in determining the intersection of query ranges and buckets, bucketization schemes are highly efficient. Based on bucketization schemes, various new approaches have been developed, including order-preserving bucketization schemes [11] and indexed bucketization schemes [12]. These bucketization schemes further enhance the efficiency of ciphertext retrieval. Currently, scholars are still conducting in-depth research on bucketization schemes and integrating them extensively with other approaches to address a variety of issues, such as security concerns, efficiency problems, and more. However, bucketization schemes have a common, unresolved problem to date, which is that they return all the ciphertexts within a bucket as query results. This data processing mechanism (where all the data in a bucket is encrypted and searched as a unit) leads to the possibility of a large number of false positive errors in query results.

The query method based on Bloom filters is a technique used to quickly determine whether an element belongs to a set. It maps elements to multiple positions in a bit array through hash functions. When querying an element, the system checks the corresponding positions in the bit array. If all positions are set to 1, it can be inferred that the element may exist in the set. If any position is 0, it can be determined that the element definitely does not belong to the set. Although Bloom filters offer efficient query speeds and low memory consumption, due to hash collisions, they can result in a certain false positive rate, where some elements are incorrectly identified as belonging to the set. This is known as "false positive" errors. Using Bloom filters for ciphertext querying is a highly efficient approach. However, Bloom filters have a certain probability of including some false positive errors in the query result range. Therefore, the query results returned by Bloom filters are not accurate [13].

3 Background Knowledge

3.1 Prefix Encoding

Prefix encoding converts a data a into a set A and converts a range $[b_1, b_2]$ into a set B. One can judge whether $a \in [b_1, b_2]$ or $a \notin [b_1, b_2]$ by determining whether $A \cap B \neq \emptyset$ or $A \cap B = \emptyset$. This property of prefix encoding is used to perform range query over plaintexts in [14]. Specifically, a data a is firstly converted into its binary string form, denoted by $a_1a_2...a_l$ (l is the length of the binary string form of a). Then, the binary string form $a_1a_2...a_l$ is converted into its prefix code set $P(a) = \{a_1a_2...a_{l-1}a_l, a_1a_2...a_{l-1}*, a_1a_2...**, a_1*...**, **...**\}$. In this prefix code set, there are $l + 1$ elements and the symbol $*$ can be the bit 0 or the bit 1. The range $[m, n]$ (b_1 and b_2 should also be converted into l length binary strings) is converted into its prefix code set, denoted by $P([m, n])$. $P([m, n])$ is the smallest set that can cover all elements in the range. If $a \in [m, n]$, there must be $P(a) \cap P([m, n]) \neq \emptyset$.

For example, 5 is a positive integer. The binary string form of 5 is $(101)_2$. Thus, the prefix code set of 5 is $P(5) = \{101, 10*, 1**, ***\}$. Given a range $[2, 6]$, the prefix code set of the range $[2, 6]$ is $P([2, 6]) = \{010, 011, 100, 101, 110\}$. As (1) 010 and 011 can be merged into $01*$, (2) 100 and 101 can be merged into $10*$, $P([2, 6]) = \{01*, 10*, 110\}$. As $5 \in [2, 6]$, there must be $P(5) \cap P([2, 6]) \neq \emptyset[2, 6]) \neq \emptyset$.

3.2 Bilinear Groups

G and G_T are two multiplicative cyclic groups of prime order p. g is a generator of G and $e : G \times G \rightarrow G_T$ is a bilinear map with following properties:

(1) Bilinearity: for all $u, v \in G$ and $a, b \in Z_p$, we have $e(u^a, v^b) = e(u, v)^{ab}$;
(2) Non-degeneracy: $e(g, g) \neq 1$.

The group operation in G and the bilinear map $e : G \times G \rightarrow G_T$ are efficiently computable.

3.3 Bloom Filter

Bloom filter [13] offers a probabilistic but very efficient method to determine whether an element belongs to a set. A Bloom filter contains (1) a set $E = \{e_1, e_2, ..., e_n\}$ (n is a positive integer), (2) a hash function *hash* and w different hash keys $k_1, k_2, ..., k_w$ (w is a positive integer), (3) a bit array A of t bits (each bit is initialize to 0). For each element $e_i \in E$ ($i = 1, 2, ..., n$), the Bloom filter computes hash values $hash(e_i, k_1)$, $hash(e_i, k_2), ..., hash(e_i, k_w)$, and then sets the values at the positions $hash(e_i, k_1)$, $hash(e_i, k_2), ..., hash(e_i, k_w)$ of A to 1. To test whether an element e' belongs to the set E, the Bloom filter calculates the hash values $hash(e', k_1), hash(e', k_2), ..., hash(e', k_w)$. If all the values at the positions $hash(e', k_1), hash(e', k_2), ..., hash(e', k_w)$ of A are 1, e' is considered to be a member of E. Otherwise, e' is not in E.

4 System Model

The system model of our scheme showed in Fig. 1 includs three roles. Firstly, the data owner generates a secure index and encrypts all the numeric data. Secondly, the data owner outsources the secure index and the ciphertexts of the numeric data to the cloud server. Thirdly, the data owner generates secret parameters and distributes them to a data user. Then, by using the secret parameters, the data user generates query token according to his/her queried range and distributes the query token to the cloud server. Finally, the cloud server performs the queried range on the secure index and sends the retrieved ciphertexts to the data user as the query results. The entire process is direct and efficient, which greatly helps improve query accuracy.

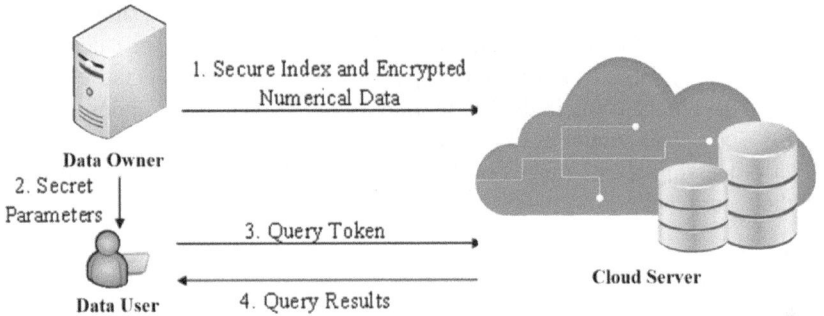

Fig. 1. System Model

Definition 1. (Security [15]) Given a leakage function F, all adversaries A cannot reveal more information except the leakage function F, then the order preserving encryption scheme is secure. The leakage function F is defined as $F(m_i, m_j) = position_{diff}(m_i, m_j)$, where $position_{diff}(m_i, m_j)$ gives the different first position of m_i and m_j.

5   Construction of Our Scheme

In this section, we firstly represent the construction method for the secure index. Then, we introduce the generation of query token in detail. Finally, we illustrate the range query on the secure index, and explain how the query performance has been improved.

5.1   Secure Index Generation

The secure index is an ordered binary tree. Each node of the secure index is associated with a range. All the nodes at the same level of the secure index are linked in an ordered manner according to their ranges. For ease of explanation, we suppose N is a node of the secure index and N is associated with the range $[m, n]$. Firstly, the data owner converts m into its binary string form, denoted by $m_1 m_2 ... m_l$ (l is the length of the binary string form of m)◦ Secondly, the data owner pads a random number r_m after m. Specifically, the data owner converts r_m into its binary string form, denoted by $r_{m_1} r_{m_2} ... r_{m_l}$, and then pads $r_{m_1} r_{m_2} ... r_{m_l}$ after $m_1 m_2 ... m_l$, denoted by $m_1 m_2 ... m_l r_{m_1} r_{m_2} ... r_{m_l}$. By using the same method, the data owner calculates the binary string form of n and pads a random number r_n after n, denoted by $n_1 n_2 ... n_l r_{n_1} r_{n_2} ... r_{n_l}$. Then, the data owner merges all the binary strings from $m_1 m_2 ... m_l r_{m_1} r_{m_2} ... r_{m_l}$ to $n_1 n_2 ... n_l r_{n_1} r_{n_2} ... r_{n_l}$. Next, the data owner obtains a prefix code set $P([m, n])$ by using the symbol $*$ (the symbol $*$ can be the bit 0 or the bit 1). Thus, $P([m, n])$ only contains several binary strings.

For example, we suppose $[0, 2]$ is the range which should be processed. The binary string of 0 is 00. The binary string of 2 is 10. 3 is a random number for 00 and the binary string of 3 is 11. 1 is a random number for 10 and the binary string of 1 is 01. Thus, all the binary strings from 0011 to 1001 should be merged together by using the symbol $*$. Thus, after randomization, the prefix code set of the range $[0, 2]$ is $P([0, 2]) = \{0011, 01 * *, 100*\}$.

By using the using the elements in $P([m, n])$, the data owner obtains a binary string by using the Bloom filter technique and a pair of two values by using the bilinear groups. Specifically, for each element $e_i \in P([m, n])$, the data owner calculates hash values $hash(e_i, k_1), hash(e_i, k_2), ..., hash(e_i, k_w)$, and sets the values at these hash value positions of the binary string in the Bloom filter to 1. The data owner chooses a random number r_{e_i} for e_i, and computes two values $g^{r_{e_i} \cdot e_i}$ and $g^{r_{e_i}}$.

After processing all the ranges of the nodes of the binary tree, the data owner can obtain the secure index.

5.2   Query Token Generation

On the situation that the data user quires a range $[p, q]$. Firstly, the data user converts p into its binary string form, denoted by $p_1 p_2 ... p_l$. Secondly, the data user chooses a random number r_p, and computes its binary string form, denoted by $r_{p_1} r_{p_2}...r_{p_l}$. Thirdly, the data user pads $r_{p_1} r_{p_2}...r_{p_l}$ after $p_1 p_2...p_l$, denoted by $p_1 p_2...p_l r_{p_1} r_{p_2}...r_{p_l}$. Then, the data user calculates the prefix code set $P(p) = \{p_1 p_2...p_l r_{p_1} r_{p_2}...r_{p_l}, p_1 p_2...p_l r_{p_1} r_{p_2}...*, ..., * *$ $...*\}$. For each element $e_p \in P(p)$, the data user calculates hash values $hash(e_p, k_1)$, $hash(e_p, k_2),..., hash(e_p, k_w)$. Next, the data user chooses a random number r_{e_p}, and calculates two values $g^{r_{ep} \cdot e_p}$ and $g^{r_{ep}}$ by using the bilinear groups. By using the same method, the data user calculates $P(q)$, the hash values of the elements in $P(q)$, and calculates $g^{r_{eq} \cdot e_q}$ and $g^{r_{eq}}$, where e_q is an element in $P(q)$ and r_{e_q} is a random number chosen for e_q. Finally, the data user sends the hash values of each element e_p in $P(p)$, the corresponding values $g^{r_{ep} \cdot e_p}$ and $g^{r_{ep}}$, the hash values of each element e_q in $P(q)$, the corresponding values $g^{r_{eq} \cdot e_q}$ and $g^{r_{eq}}$ to the cloud server as the query token.

5.3 Range Query

After receiving the query token from the data user, for each element $e_p \in P(p)$, the cloud server extracts the hash values $hash(e_p, k_1)$, $hash(e_p, k_2),..., hash(e_p, k_w)$ from the query token (note that e_p is an element in $P(p)$ and $P(p)$ contains several elements). If there exists an element e_p that the values at the positions $hash(e_p, k_1)$, $hash(e_p, k_2),...,$ $hash(e_p, k_w)$ of the binary string are 1, which are stored in the node of the secure index, and also they are generated by using Bloom filter. Then it is easy to know that p is considered to be in the range of the node. Otherwise, p is not in the range of the node. For an ease way to explain, we suppose the values at the positions $hash(e_p, k_1)$, $hash(e_p, k_2),...,$ $hash(e_p, k_w)$ of the binary string (generated by using Bloom filter) stored in the node of the secure index are 1. According to Bloom filter technique, p is within the range of the node with a certain probability (false positives may occur in Bloom filter). The cloud server determines whether $e(g^{r_{ei} \cdot e_i}, g^{r_{ep}}) = e(g^{r_{ep} \cdot e_p}, g^{r_{ei}})$. If the equation holds, there is $e_i = e_p$, which means $P([m, n]) \cap P(p) \neq \emptyset$. Thus, there is $p \in [m, n]$. By using the same method, the cloud server can determine whether $q \in [m, n]$.

In a top-down manner, the cloud server can find two leaf nodes. The range of a leaf node covers p, and the range of the other leaf node covers q. As the leaf nodes of the secure index is ordered, thus the cloud server can efficiently retrieve all the encrypted numeric data from the secure index. Finally, the cloud server returns all the retrieved ciphertexts to the data user as the query results.

Note that, as Bloom filter is adopted, the cloud server can perform range query very efficient. Meanwhile, as bilinear mapping is adopted, the cloud server can exclude the false positives in the query results.

6 Security Analysis

Theorem 1. The proposed scheme is secure with respect to the leak function F.

Proof 1. Suppose that there are two numbers $a = a_1 a_2...a_n$ and $b = b_1 b_2...b_n$ after padding, if the number of members in the intersection of $P(a)$ and $P(b)$ is m, it can deduce that $a_1 = b_1$, $a_2 = b_2$, ..., $a_{m-1} = b_{m-1}$, $a_m \neq b_m$. Therefore, the cloud server only knows the leakage function $F(m_i, m_j) = position_{diff}(m_i, m_j)$. In summary, our scheme is secure with respect to leakage function F.

7 Experiments

In our experiments, we conducted a thorough examination of the efficiency of our proposed scheme. This scheme is intricately designed based on a combination of prefix encoding, Bloom filters, and bilinear group operations. The implementation of bilinear group operations was facilitated through the Java Pairing Based Cryptography Library version 2.0.0 [16].

To evaluate the performance of our scheme, we employed the method of controlling variables to analyze two key properties: the height of the secure index and the ratio between the query scale and the data range. By systematically varying these parameters, we were able to gauge the impact of these factors on the efficiency of our scheme.

Our experiments were carried out on a Windows 10 computer system equipped with an AMD Ryzen 5 2500U processor and 8GB of RAM (Random Access Memory). This setup provided the computational resources necessary to execute our experiments effectively and to collect precise data on the performance metrics of our scheme under different conditions. The choice of hardware ensured a stable testing environment for evaluating the efficiency and scalability of our proposed solution in handling encrypted numerical data in a cloud setting.

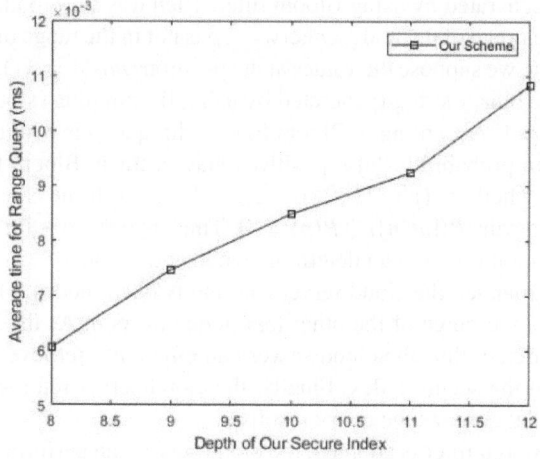

Fig. 2. Range Query Time with the Depth of Secure Index

As shown in Fig. 2, the range query on the secure index is highly efficient. The query time increases linearly with the data size. This efficiency is attributed to the highly efficient comparison mechanism of the Bloom filter, with the number of comparisons increasing only with the index height. Consequently, even as the data volume grows, the query efficiency can be maintained, allowing this querying method to exhibit strong performance on large-scale datasets. This capability provides reliable support for data retrieval and processing.

As shown in Fig. 3, we set the height of the secure index to 12 and expanded the query range. As the ratio of the query range to the data range increases, the query time

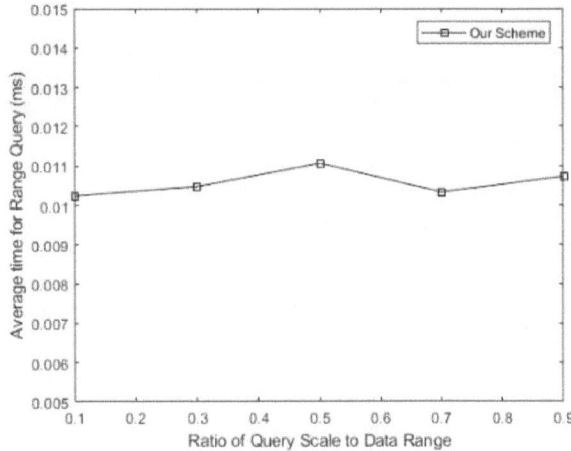

Fig. 3. Range Query Time with the Ratio of Query Scale to Data Range

remains unchanged. This is because, during range queries on the secure index, the cloud server only needs to compare the two endpoints of the query range with the index nodes, without increasing the number of comparisons as the query range expands. This keeps the computational complexity constant during the query process, resulting in consistent query times. This design excels in handling large-scale datasets, providing faster and more reliable support for data retrieval and processing.

8 Conclusions

We have proposed a fast and accurate query scheme for encrypted numerical data in a cloud environment. Compared to order-preserving encryption schemes [9], we protect the ordering information of the encrypted numerical data by sorting only the ranges in the secure index (thus safeguarding the ordering information of the encrypted numerical data covered by these ranges). Unlike traditional bucketization schemes [10], data users do not need to store index information on their side. In comparison to order-preserving bucketization schemes [11], index bucketization schemes [12], and public key-based encryption schemes [2, 17], our approach employs a combination of Bloom filters and bilinear group operations. This enhances the efficiency of the query process and ensures that query results do not contain any false positives.

In our experiments, we have validated the effectiveness of this approach. Results indicate that our query scheme maintains efficiency and accuracy when handling large-scale datasets. As the query range expands, the query time remains stable, thanks to the outstanding performance of the Bloom filters and bilinear group operations utilized in our approach. This design advantage positions our scheme as a reliable solution for data security and privacy protection when processing encrypted numerical data queries in a cloud environment. Additionally, we have conducted rigorous proofs and analyses of the security of our scheme.

References

1. Feng, J., Yang, L.T., Zhu, Q., Choo, K.-K.R.: Privacy-preserving tensor decomposition over encrypted data in a federated cloud environment. IEEE Trans. Dependable Secure Comput. **17**(4), 857–868 (2020)
2. Mei, Z., Yu, J., Zhang, C., et al.: Secure multi-dimensional data retrieval with access control and range query in the cloud. Inf. Syst. **122**, 102343 (2024)
3. Feng, J., Yang, L.T., Ren, B., Zou, D., Dong, M., Zhang, S.: Tensor recurrent neural network with differential privacy. IEEE Trans. Comput. **73**(3), 683–693 (2024)
4. Zhang, S., Yang, L.T., Kuang, L., Feng, J., Chen, J., Piuri, V.: A tensor-based forensics framework for virtualized network functions in the internet of things: utilizing tensor algebra in facilitating more efficient network forensic investigations. IEEE Consum. Electron. Magaz. **8**(3), 23–27 (2019)
5. Wu, Z., Xie, J., Shen, S., Lin, C., Xu, G., Chen, E.: A confusion method for the protection of user topic privacy in Chinese keyword-based book retrieval. ACM Trans. Asian Low-resource Lang. Inf. Process. **22**(5), 1–19 (2023)
6. Wu, Z., Li, G., Shen, S., Lian, X., Chen, E., Xu, G.: Constructing dummy query sequences to protect location privacy and query privacy in location-based services. World Wide Web **24**, 25–49 (2021)
7. Wu, Z., Shen, S., Li, H., Zhou, H., Lu, C.: A basic framework for privacy protection in personalized information retrieval: an effective framework for user privacy protection. J. Organiz. End User Comput. **33**(6), 1–26 (2021)
8. Wu, Z., Liu, H., Xie, J., Xu, G., Li, G., Lu, C.: An effective method for the protection of user health topic privacy for health information services. World Wide Web, 1–23 (2023)
9. Boldyreva, A., Chenette, N., Lee, Y., O'neill, A.: Order-preserving symmetric encryption. In: Annual International Conference on the Theory and Applications of Cryptographic Techniques, pp. 224–241. Springer, Heidelberg (2009). https://doi.org/10.1007/978-3-642-01001-9_13
10. Hore, B., Mehrotra, S., Tsudik, G.: A privacy-preserving index for range queries, In: Proceedings of the Thirtieth International Conference on Very Large Data Bases, vol. 30, pp. 720–731 (2004)
11. Lee, Y.: Secure ordered bucketization. IEEE Trans. Dependable Secure Comput. **11**(3), 292–303 (2014)
12. Wang, P., Ravishankar, C.V.: Secure and efficient range queries on outsourced databases using Rp-trees. In: 2013 IEEE 29th International Conference on Data Engineering, ICDE, pp. 314–325. IEEE (2013)
13. Bloom, B.H.: Space/time trade-offs in hash coding with allowable errors. Commun. ACM **13**(7), 422–426 (1970)
14. Gupta, P., McKeown, N.: Algorithms for packet classification. IEEE Network **15**, 24–32 (2001)
15. Guo, J., Wang, J., Zhang, Z., Chen, X.: An almost non-interactive order preserving encryption scheme. In: International Conference on Information Security Practice and Experience, pp. 87–100. Springer, Cham (2018). https://doi.org/10.1007/978-3-319-99807-7_6
16. The Java Pairing Based Cryptography Library (jPBC). http://gas.dia.unisa.it/projects/jpbc/index.html. Accessed 9 Aug 2024
17. Mei, Z., Zhu, H., Cui, Z., et al.: Executing multi-dimensional range query efficiently and flexibly over outsourced ciphertexts in the cloud. Inf. Sci. **432**, 79–96 (2018)

Asynchronous I/O Persistence for In-Memory Database Servers: Leveraging io_uring to Optimize Redis Persistence

Le-Gao Chen[1]([⊠]) [iD], Yanzhi Li[2], Tipporn Laohakangvalvit[1], and Midori Sugaya[2]

[1] Innovative Global Program, College of Engineering, Shibaura Institute of Technology, Koto City, Tokyo, Japan
am21001@shibaura-it.ac.jp
[2] Department of Computer Science and Engineering, College of Engineering, Shibaura Institute of Technology, Koto City, Tokyo, Japan

Abstract. With constant hardware improvements allowing for increasingly large memory sizes, in-memory database servers have become an attractive option for various cloud applications. Even though in-memory database servers store all data in memory, there is still a need to persist data onto an I/O device for maintenance, updates, or protection against server crashes. In high throughput environments, persistence happens often, significantly hindering server throughput performance. Although popular in-memory database servers such as Redis or Dragonfly DB have adopted asynchronous I/O for socket operations, none have extended this approach for persistence. This results in significantly longer time taken for persistence, leading to prolonged reduced throughput. Given the recent introduction of io_uring, which has demonstrated significant performance improvements over past asynchronous I/O APIs, we have decided to implement it into Redis to evaluate its effectiveness in reducing these performance overheads. Our findings indicate that io_uring can significantly enhance performance in use cases with medium to large payload sizes but may hinder performances in use cases involving small payload sizes due to higher complexity and higher operation cost per datapoint. This method can likely be applied to other servers, such as Dragonfly DB and Memcached, to achieve similar benefits in appropriate scenarios. Additionally, in-memory database server persistence can serve as valuable benchmarks for further io_uring development and optimization.

Keywords: In-memory Database · Asynchronous I/O · io_uring · Redis · Data Persistence · Server Performance · Cloud Storage · YCSB

1   Introduction

With steadily decreasing memory prices, constant advancements in DDRRAM (Double Data Rate Random Access Memory) technology, and server CPU supporting more memory lanes, in-memory database servers, where all data is stored in memory as opposed to I/O devices, have started to see adoption in cloud services such as Netflix [1], Twitter

Y. Wang and L.-J. Zhang (Eds.): CLOUD 2024, LNCS 15423, pp. 11–20, 2025.
https://doi.org/10.1007/978-3-031-77153-8_2

[2], Amazon [3], Cloudflare [4], PayPal [5], and more. Compared to traditional database servers, in-memory database servers generally provide superior storage speed, retrieval speed, latency, and throughput at the cost of persistence and storage space.

One notable drawback of in-memory database servers is that because data resides solely in memory, any server downtime will result in the complete loss of all stored data. One way to fix this problem is to persist the entire database onto an I/O device periodically. While some in-memory database server solutions such as Redis [6, 7] or Dragonfly DB [8] support some form of persistence, other server solutions such as Memcached [9] do not. However, enabling this feature greatly hinders the server's performance. In our preliminary work, we have observed that when persistence operations start, throughput drops significantly for Redis. Similarly, Garcia-Molina et al. have also observed this phenomenon on other in-memory database servers [10].

This study aims to explore a potential solution to the performance degradation experienced during persistence. To achieve this goal, we have implemented io_uring [11, 12], a newly introduced asynchronous I/O API, into Redis, currently the most popular open-source in-memory database server, to observe the potential benefits and drawbacks of an asynchronous I/O path implementation of persistence for all in-memory database servers. We have also used YCSB [13] to analyze this implementation further.

2 Background

2.1 In-Memory Database Server Persistence

There are two main types of persistence for in-memory database servers: append-only file (AOF) and snapshotting [6, 7]. AOF generally refers to every command being saved onto a file on an I/O device as the server processes it. This type of persistence has three downsides. First, it slightly hinders performance throughout the entire runtime of the server. Second, it takes significantly longer for the server to reconstruct the database when restarting. Third, it takes up significantly larger space on the I/O device itself.

The second main type of persistence is snapshotting, which refers to the server periodically taking a snapshot of the database at a specific moment in time and then writing the entire database into a singular file on an I/O device. Snapshotting's main downside is the significant dip in throughput during the persistence operation. Although both types of persistence could be improved with an asynchronous I/O path, our focus for this research is snapshotting since it is more widely supported compared to AOF persistence.

Generally, snapshotting starts with the server creating a child process via either a fork or a new thread; this allows minimal interference with the main server database while the child thread works on persistence [6, 7]. Usually, these child processes use copy-on-write to not create extra memory overhead when possible [6, 7]. This child processes and then iterates through every data point in the database, saving each data point one by one [6, 7]. Currently, this saving process utilizes a synchronous I/O path where a system call is made to tell the kernel to write onto the I/O device while the child process waits for a response before continuing to the following data point [6, 7]. Synchronous I/O path results in delays between when the I/O device finishes one operation and when it starts the next. This was never really a problem in the past due to slow storage devices being the primary bottleneck. However, with advancements in storage devices resulting in affordable, stable, and high I/O per second (IOPS) I/O devices such as Samsung Z-SSD [14], Intel Optane SSD [15], and Toshiba XL-Flash [16], synchronous I/O have become one of the main bottlenecks for achieving faster persistence time.

Server applications such as Redis [6, 7], MongoDB [17], Dragonfly DB [8], VoltDB [18], Hazelcast [19], and custom Memcached [9, 20] all support snapshot persistence. Thus, our asynchronous persistence method could theoretically be implemented into these servers with minimal changes.

2.2   Linux Asynchronous I/O Paths

Asynchronous I/O path solves eliminates this delay by allowing the application to queue I/O requests and then move on to other operations immediately without waiting for a completion notice from the I/O device. This also allows the I/O device to work from one queued request to the next without waiting for an I/O request issued by the application. Generally, asynchronous I/O paths allow applications to achieve minimal CPU idle time and I/O device idle time, resulting in significantly better performance but at the cost of managing the I/O request queue. Currently, there are three implementations of an asynchronous I/O path for the Linux kernel, each with their own benefits and tradeoffs. POSIX AIO [21] is an implementation that mainly runs in the user space, utilizing user-level libraries to create dedicated I/O threads to achieve asynchronous execution. POSIX AIO's high-level implementation allows it to be compatible with all POSIX-compliant OS at the cost of significant user space overheads [21]. Kernel AIO [11, 22] is an implementation explicitly made for the Linux kernel, allowing asynchronous I/O operations to be handled directly within the kernel space. This implementation greatly reduces overheads associated with user-space context switching and thread management, resulting in significantly better performance. However, with the advent of high IOPS devices in high throughput applications, traditional approaches like POSIX AIO [21] and Kernel AIO [11, 22] have begun to show their limitations, thus leading to the development of io_uring [11, 12].

io_uring [11, 12] is the newest asynchronous I/O interface with significant improvements over Kernel AIO in terms of both performance and features. io_uring introduces a more streamlined and efficient architecture by using a dual ring buffers system for the submission and completion of I/O requests, resulting in drastically reduced system call overhead and minimized context switching. Although io_uring is still under scrutiny for its stability, security, and compatibility [23], given that it has entirely overhauled the asynchronous I/O path, its potential significantly surpassed other asynchronous I/O methods. Therefore, the implementation discussed in this paper will be leveraging io_uring.

3   Our Implementation of Asynchronous I/O Persistence

3.1   Analysis of Redis Persistence

We have chosen Redis for our implementation and testing due to its popularity [24], simplicity, and stability. Other servers, such as DragonflyDB, which includes a snapshot feature for persistence, generally operate very similarly to Redis [6, 8, 17–20, 25] thus we can expect the same benefits and drawbacks for asynchronous I/O persistence on other servers.

Redis' snapshot persistence function begins with a fork, creating a child process with the copy-on-write mechanism dedicated to the persistence task. This child process then iterates over each data point in the database, sequentially saving each data point's type, key, and value. After the data point is written onto disk, the data point is then freed from memory to reduce memory overhead. When the child process successfully saves the snapshot, it is then terminated. This simple mechanism for snapshot persistence presents a perfect system for modification.

3.2   Utilizing io_uring for Asynchronous Persistence

We kept the implementation as straightforward as possible to fully reflect the current performance of io_uring while minimizing potential overheads. Our implementation utilizes a feature called SQPOLL [26], where a thread is created specifically to poll for requests submitted to the submission queue.

There are three key challenges we faced when integrating asynchronous I/O via the io_uring API into Redis. First, writing with a synchronous I/O path guarantees that once the write request is issued, the thread would be blocked until its completion allowing the associated data buffers to be safely freed immediately. However, with an asynchronous I/O path, the data is not immediately written, it is submitted to a submission queue where the operation will be carried out later. This introduces a significant problem where we cannot free the data buffers after submitting the write requests as they need to remain available until the I/O operation completes. Another issue we encountered was managing the limited space available in the submission queue. With large databases the submission queue can quickly become full. Without proper queue management, this could cause the submission of write requests to block, or even cause write requests to fail. Lastly, since the child process responsible for snapshot persistence cannot terminate until all pending write requests are completed, we need a mechanism to ensure that the process waits for all write operations to finish before it can safely exit.

To solve the first problem, we implemented a solution that attaches a data pointer to the submission request so that we can safely free the data point once the confirmation is received as illustrated in Fig. 1, ensuring the data will not be freed prematurely. To solve the second problem, we poll the completion queue to keep track of the number of completed requests as opposed to the number of submitted requests, ensuring sufficient space before submitting new requests. To solve the last problem, we implemented a clean-up process which starts after all written requests are submitted. This clean-up process polls the completion queue until all requests are completed before allowing the child process to end.

For clarity, we will refer to our implementation as "uring Redis" throughout the remainder of this paper. io_uring persistence structure between the application and the kernel space is illustrated in Fig. 1. The overlapping effect of asynchronous I/O between the CPU and the I/O device is illustrated in Fig. 2.

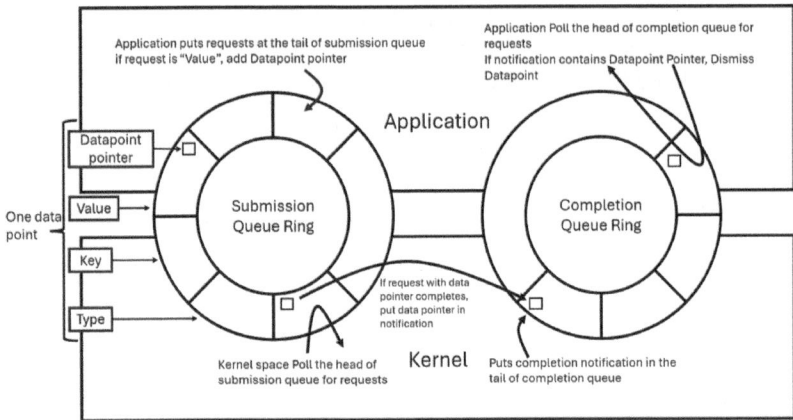

Fig. 1. io_uring queue structure for Redis persistence

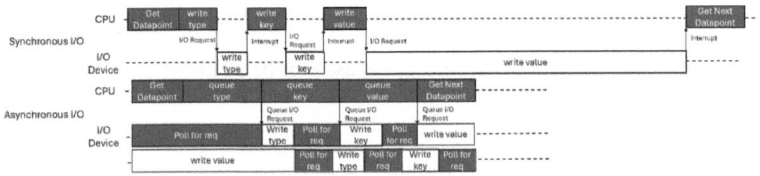

Fig. 2. A sequence diagram of synchronous persistence and asynchronous persistence.

4 Evaluation Methods and Metrics

4.1 Evaluation Method

We utilized a standardized tool for database server benchmarking, Yahoo! Cloud Serving Benchmark or YCSB [13], to evaluate our implementation. The tests consist of three different workloads with three different payload sizes. The three workloads consisting of Read, Update, and Read Modify Write (RMW) commands, are described in Table 1, and the three payload sizes are described in Table 2. These workloads are partially inspired by database benchmarks done by Seghier et al. [27]. In total, we have nine benchmarks for each server to fully evaluate the benefits and drawbacks of io_uring [11, 12] on database server persistence. We ran each test five times to ensure consistency. All tests were done on the computer described in Table 3.

4.2 Metrics

There are two phases to a YCSB workload. First is the load phase, where the benchmark loads the server with the benchmark database. Second is the test phase, where the benchmark is conducted [13]. The load phase consists of only insert commands, whereas the test phase contains different types of commands listed above in Table 1. Average throughput and average time taken for persistence during the entire test is recorded and analyzed.

Table 1. Workloads

Workload ID	Read	Update	RMW
W(a)	50%	50%	0%
W(b)	95%	5%	0%
W(c)	50%	0%	50%

Table 2. Payloads

Payload ID	Sizes
P(a)	32 kilobytes
P(b)	64 kilobytes
P(c)	128 kilobytes

Table 3. Computer specs used for benchmarks

Component	Specs
CPU	AMD Ryzen 7 7700x
RAM	32 GB DDR5-6000 MHz (2x16 GB)
SSD	Samsung 980 1 TB
OS	Fedora Linux 38 6.5.10-200.fc38.x86_64
Redis	Version 7.2.4

5 Results

During tests with payload sizes of 32 kb, traditional Redis consistently finished persistence around five seconds faster than uring Redis. During tests with payload sizes of 64 kb, both servers took around the same amount of time for persistence. During tests with payload sizes of 128 kb, uring Redis saved 3 s faster than traditional Redis [7] as shown in Fig. 3. This speed difference led to uring Redis persisting one additional time within the test period for tests with payload size of 128 kb, which negatively hindered throughput. While traditional Redis' time taken for persistence seemed to not be affected by the different tests, uring Redis' performance is greatly affected by the payload size of the specific test.

For the testing phase, traditional Redis consistently slightly outperformed uring Redis for tests with payload sizes of 32 kb and 64 kb, as indicated in Fig. 4. For tests with 128 kb, uring Redis was expected to outperform traditional Redis slightly. However, due to an additional persistence operation caused by the significantly faster time taken for persistence, it ultimately performed slightly worse.

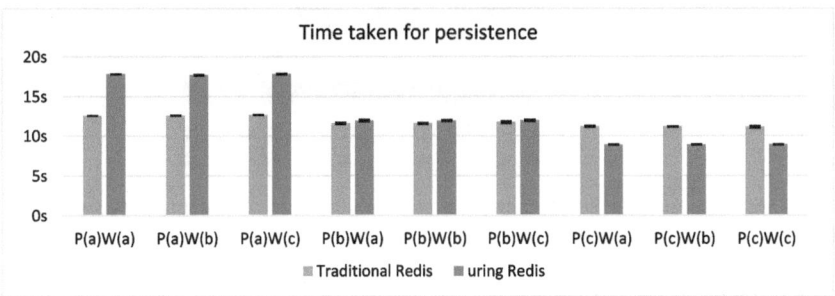

Fig. 3. Average time taken for persistence throughout all tests.

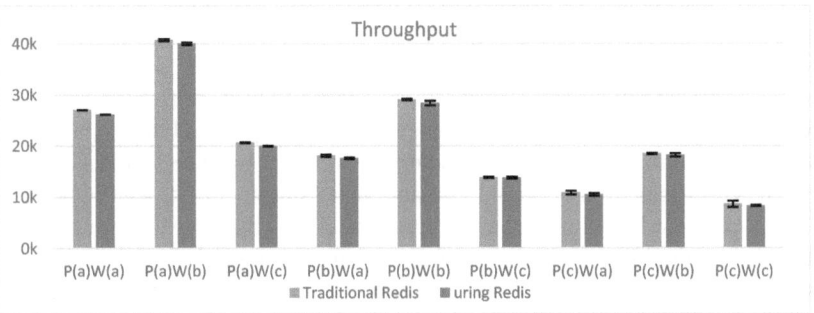

Fig. 4. Average throughput during the testing phase of YCSB.

6 Discussion

6.1 Asynchronous I/O Persistence Potential

Although the test results do not favor our implementation, the significance of a 3 s reduction in time taken for persistence should not be overlooked. One of the benefits we can confirm from our tests is the shortened interval between persistence operations, resulting in uring Redis persisting one additional time for payload sizes with 128 kb. If the additional persistence is removed, we could theoretically see better throughput for uring Redis than traditional Redis [7].

6.2 Reason for Underperformance

The reason for this underperformance for tests with a payload size of 32 kb may be due to significantly less overlap between I/O device operations and CPU operations when payload sizes are small, as shown in Fig. 5. When this happens, there are no benefits to using asynchronous I/O, resulting in significantly worse performance. This effect is magnified in Redis persistence specifically because the type of the data point only takes up 1 byte but still needs to be queued in the same way as key and value. Which results in uring Redis performance being greatly dependent on the payload size of the tests.

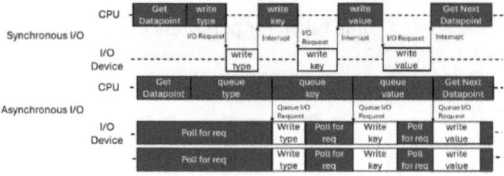

Fig. 5. A sequence diagram showing the degradation of Asynchronous I/O performance under workloads with small payload sizes

6.3   Potential Improvements and Future Work

Several io_uring features [11, 12] and asynchronous I/O techniques could greatly enhance the performance of uring Redis. First, to solve the issue of extremely small requests such as type, request merging could be used to send big blocks of smaller requests, resulting in potentially significantly better performance [28]. Second, since the buffers in Redis are not memory-aligned, we cannot use high-performance parameters like O_DIRECT and IO_POLLING. However, by aligning these buffers in memory, it would be possible to enable these parameters and thereby enhance performance. Third, there is recent research on an NVMe passthrough using io_uring, where the application can bypass the kernel and communicate directly to the NVMe device [29]. This can be used to significantly lower resource consumption and latency incurred by the kernel space. However, it would also require a complete overhaul of the persistence database structure, the persistence operation, and the reconstruction of the database. Lastly, since io_uring [11, 12, 23] is still under development, we may see significantly better performance if they are able to lower the overheads specified in this research.

7   Conclusion

The implementation of io_uring [11, 12] in Redis [6, 7] demonstrates a promising advancement in optimizing persistence for in-memory database servers. This approach significantly improved the persistence performance of large payload sizes. Due to the complexity and operational overheads, the performance of smaller payload sizes is significantly reduced. However, with the potential implementation of other techniques in addition to io_uring [11, 12], such as request merging [28], memory alignment, and NVMe passthrough [29], the performance of io_uring persistence may improve greatly.

These results suggest that while io_uring [11, 12] offers potential for optimizing persistence for in-memory database servers, its application must be carefully considered based on the workload characteristics, and that several challenges regarding overheads need to be addressed before this implementation can be utilized in widely cloud servers.

References

1. Netflix Technology Blog. Timestone: Netflix's high-throughput, low-latency priority queueing system with built-in support (2022). https://netflixtechblog.com/timestone-net flixs-high-throughput-low-latency-priority-queueing-system-with-built-in-support-1abf24 9ba95f. Accessed 12 Aug 2024

2. X Engineering Blog. Caching with Twemcache (2012). https://blog.x.com/engineering/en_us/a/2012/caching-with-twemcache. Accessed 12 Aug 2024

3. Amazon Web Services. What is Amazon ElastiCache for Memcached? (n.d.). https://docs.aws.amazon.com/AmazonElastiCache/latest/mem-ug/WhatIs.html. Accessed 12 Aug 2024

4. Cloudflare Blog. Why we started putting unpopular assets in memory (2020). https://blog.cloudflare.com/why-we-started-putting-unpopular-assets-in-memory/. Accessed 12 Aug 2024

5. Aerospike. PayPal: Fraud prevention with data (n.d.). https://aerospike.com/resources/case-study/paypal-fraud-prevention-with-data/. Accessed 12 Aug 2024

6. Redis Documentation. Persistence (n.d.). https://redis.io/docs/latest/operate/oss_and_stack/management/persistence/. Accessed 12 Aug 2024

7. Redis. Redis 7.2.4 [Source code]. GitHub (2023). https://github.com/redis/redis/releases/tag/7.2.4

8. DragonflyDB Documentation. Backups (n.d.). https://www.dragonflydb.io/docs/managing-dragonfly/backups. Accessed 12 Aug 2024

9. Memcached. Memcached. GitHub repository (n.d.). https://github.com/memcached/memcached. Accessed 12 Aug 2024

10. Garcia-Molina, H., Salem, K.: Main memory database systems: an overview. IEEE Trans. Knowl. Data Eng. **4**(6), 509–516 (1992)

11. Nell, P., Hofstede, R., Tanenbaum, A S.: Understanding modern storage APIs: a systematic study of libaio, SPDK, and io_uring (2022). https://research.vu.nl/ws/portalfiles/portal/217956662/Understanding_Modern_Storage_APIs_A_systematic_study_of_libaio_SPDK_and_io_uring.pdf. Accessed 12 Aug 2024

12. Axboe, J.: io_uring. (2019). https://kernel.dk/io_uring.pdf. Accessed 12 Aug 2024

13. Cooper, B.F.: YCSB: Yahoo! Cloud Serving Benchmark. GitHub repository. (n.d.). https://github.com/brianfrankcooper/YCSB. Accessed 12 Aug 2024

14. Samsung. Ultra-low Latency with Samsung Z-NAND SSD. (n.d.). https://download.semiconductor.samsung.com/resources/brochure/Ultra-Low%20Latency%20with%20Samsung%20Z-NAND%20SSD.pdf. Accessed 12 Aug 2024

15. Intel. Intel® Optane™ SSD 905P series product brief. (n.d.). https://www.intel.com/content/dam/www/public/us/en/documents/product-briefs/optane-ssd-905p-product-brief.pdf. Accessed 12 Aug 2024

16. Kioxia Corporation. Kioxia introduces new technology for next-generation memory (2018). https://americas.kioxia.com/en-ca/business/news/2018/memory-20180806-1.html. Accessed 12 Aug 2024

17. MongoDB Documentation. Mongodump (n.d.). https://www.mongodb.com/docs/database-tools/mongodump/. Accessed 12 Aug 2024

18. VoltDB Documentation. SAVE: Save the contents of the database to disk (n.d.). https://docs.voltdb.com/UsingVoltDB/sysprocsave.php. Accessed 12 Aug 2024

19. Hazelcast Documentation. Persistence. (n.d.). https://docs.hazelcast.com/hazelcast/5.5/storage/persistence. Accessed 12 Aug 2024

20. Juanber84. Memcached dump. GitHub repository. (n.d.). https://github.com/juanber84/memcached-dump. Accessed 12 Aug 2024

21. IEEE Standards Association. IEEE 1003.1-2024 - IEEE/Open Group Standard for Information Technology--Portable Operating System Interface (POSIX™) Base Specifications, no. 8. IEEE Computer Society (2024). https://standards.ieee.org/ieee/1003.1/7700/

22. Crossbuild. libaio [GitHub repository]. GitHub. (n.d.). https://github.com/crossbuild/libaio/tree/master. Accessed 12 Aug 2024

23. Paul Moore. io_uring: So Fast. It's Scary. Presented at Linux Security Summit Europe. YouTube, uploaded by The Linux Foundation, 9 October (2022). https://www.youtube.com/watch?v=AaaH6skUEI8&t=1850s

24. DragonflyDB Documentation. In-memory databases guide (n.d.). https://www.dragonflydb. io/guides/in-memory-databases. Accessed 12 Aug 2024

25. DragonflyDB Documentation. In-memory architecture (n.d.). https://www.dragonflydb.io/in-memory. Accessed 12 Aug 2024

26. Unixism. SQPOLL: an introduction to polling in io_uring (n.d.). https://unixism.net/loti/tut orial/sq_poll.html. Accessed 12 Aug 2024

27. Seghier, N.B., Kazar, O.: Performance benchmarking and comparison of NoSQL databases: Redis vs MongoDB vs Cassandra using YCSB tool. In: 2021 International Conference on Recent Advances in Mathematics and Informatics (ICRAMI), pp. 1–6. Tebessa, Algeria (2021)

28. Chowdhury, M.K.H., Tang, H., Bez, J.L., Bangalore, P.V., Byna, S.: Efficient asynchronous I/O with request merging. In: 2023 IEEE International Parallel and Distributed Processing Symposium Workshops (IPDPSW), pp. 628–636. IEEE, St. Petersburg (2023)

29. Joshi, P.: Title of the presentation. In: Proceedings of the 22nd USENIX Conference on File and Storage Technologies (FAST 2024) (2024). https://www.usenix.org/conference/fast24/presentation/joshi. Accessed 12 Aug 2024

Enhancing Election Security Through Blockchain: An In-Depth Study of Encrypted NFTs and Smart Contracts

Le K. Bang[1], Hong Vo Khanh[1(⊠)], Minh Nguyen Triet[1], N. N. Hung[1],
Phung Dang Trinh[1], Hai Ngo Bang[1], Nguyen T. Anh[1],
and K. T. Nguyen Ngan[2]

[1] FPT University, Can Tho city, Vietnam
khanhvh@fe.edu.vn
[2] FPT Polytechnic, Can Tho city, Vietnam

Abstract. This paper presents a blockchain-based framework designed to address current challenges in electoral systems, including security vulnerabilities, transparency issues, and inefficiencies. By integrating blockchain technology, smart contracts, encrypted Non-Fungible Tokens (NFTs), and the InterPlanetary File System (IPFS), our system aims to enhance the security, transparency, and operational efficiency of voting processes. Through a detailed evaluation across four EVM-compatible blockchain platforms-Binance Smart Chain, Polygon, Fantom, and Celo-we assess the adaptability, performance, and economic efficiency of the proposed system. The study reveals potential benefits in using blockchain technology to manage voting records effectively, providing a secure, accessible, and efficient solution for contemporary electoral challenges.

Keywords: Blockchain Voting Systems · Electoral Integrity · EVM Platforms · Smart Contracts in Elections · NFTs for Voter Authentication

1 Introduction

Modern democratic societies depend on the reliability and integrity of their voting systems. Yet, these systems, often based on traditional practices, face increasing challenges including security vulnerabilities, transparency issues, and operational inefficiencies [10]. These problems are not just theoretical; they have been demonstrated in various incidents that have undermined public confidence in the electoral process. The integrity of elections is crucial because it directly affects the legitimacy of democratic governance [1]. The rising mistrust in these systems, fueled by technical failures and concerns about vote manipulation, underscores the critical need for a comprehensive reevaluation and modernization of the electoral process.

© The Author(s), under exclusive license to Springer Nature Switzerland AG 2025
Y. Wang and L.-J. Zhang (Eds.): CLOUD 2024, LNCS 15423, pp. 21–36, 2025.
https://doi.org/10.1007/978-3-031-77153-8_3

Blockchain technology is acknowledged for its potential to improve electoral systems, offering benefits such as immutability, decentralization, and cryptographic security that are pertinent to the requirements of a reliable voting system [2]. The immutable characteristic of blockchain ensures that once votes are logged, they cannot be altered, greatly minimizing the risks of tampering and fraud. Its decentralized nature enhances transparency and accountability [8], permitting multiple parties to validate electoral transactions while protecting voter privacy. This could substantially bolster electoral systems, enhancing their security and transparency, which are essential for rebuilding public trust in democratic processes [15]. However, while recent studies have progressed in enhancing transparency and security in blockchain-based voting systems [3,6,9,11,13], they often focus more on system design and theoretical aspects, with less emphasis on practical implementation challenges and scalability in real-world scenarios. There is a continuing need for further research into user experience and ease of use, crucial for wider acceptance.

Our proposed framework utilizes the decentralized attributes of blockchain technology, offering a secure alternative to traditional and electronic voting systems. The inherent features of blockchain, such as immutability and transparency, are particularly advantageous for managing sensitive voting data. In this system, RSA encryption, alongside other algorithms such as RC4, DES, ChaCha20, Blowfish, and AES, is integrated with Non-Fungible Tokens (NFTs) to secure the voting records, ensuring that only authorized users can access them. This method not only safeguards privacy but also maintains the uniqueness and integrity of each voter's record. Additionally, smart contracts are employed to automate the creation, access, and transfer of these records. These contracts execute terms directly programmed into their code, enhancing the security and efficiency of interactions within the electoral system, minimizing the possibility of errors, and providing a reliable mechanism for managing access to voting information.

Our proposed system's adaptability and performance were methodically assessed across four EVM-compatible blockchain platforms: Binance Smart Chain, Polygon, Fantom, and Celo. This assessment aimed to determine how effectively the system could leverage the distinct characteristics of each platform to enhance the management of voting records. We focused on essential functions such as recording voting data, creating NFTs encrypted with various algorithms (RSA, RC4, DES, ChaCha20, Blowfish, and AES) for secure record storage, and the transferability of these NFTs. These evaluations provided insights into the system's operational speed, resource efficiency, and overall reliability [12]. Additionally, we reviewed the transaction costs associated with these platforms, which offered perspectives on potential cost savings and enhanced operational efficiency for managing voting records

In conclusion, our study introduces a method that utilizes blockchain technology, smart contracts, encrypted Non-Fungible Tokens (NFTs), and the Inter-Planetary File System (IPFS) to enhance the management of voting records. This approach effectively addresses challenges associated with data security, accessibility, and integrity, thereby establishing a new benchmark for how voting records can be managed securely and efficiently. Through the application of various encryption algorithms-RSA, RC4, DES, ChaCha20, Blowfish, and AES-our research evaluates their appropriateness in terms of security and operational efficiency. We have thoroughly investigated the integration of these technologies and highlighted their potential in creating a voting management system that is secure and practical for stakeholders in the electoral sector.

2   Related Work

2.1   Blockchain and Voting System Transparency

Li et al. [9] address balancing transparency with voter privacy in blockchain-based voting systems, introducing an authority management mechanism to preserve voter confidentiality while maintaining data integrity. Similarly, Fusco et al. [3] explore integrating Shamir's secret sharing with blockchain to enhance vote privacy and auditability, aiming to secure electronic voting by ensuring both confidentiality and transparency.

Singh et al. [13] examine the use of blockchain to enhance security in digital voting systems, addressing necessary architectural and operational elements for a secure implementation. They illustrate how blockchain mitigates common electronic voting security threats, enhancing process integrity. Similarly, Khan et al. [6] explore a blockchain-based voting system that emphasizes cryptographic security to ensure a verifiable voting process. Their work demonstrates how blockchain's security features can create a more transparent and secure voting environment.

2.2   Decentralization and Privacy

Patil et al. [11] explore the use of blockchain in electronic voting, noting the advantages of decentralization and anonymity in promoting fair and unbiased elections. They highlight how blockchain ensures voter anonymity and maintains electoral integrity. Indapwar et al. [5] detail the development of a decentralized voting system where blockchain significantly reduces the risk of data tampering, thereby enhancing security and accuracy in elections. Hjalmarsson et al. [4] evaluate various blockchain frameworks for electronic voting, contributing to the development of systems that address current electronic voting challenges. Kumar et al. [7] propose increasing the transparency and security of electronic voting by using separate blockchains to store voter details and votes, which supports voter anonymity and allows for verifiable vote tallying.

2.3   Comparative Analysis of Blockchain-Based Voting Systems

This subsection situates our study within the broader landscape of blockchain-based voting systems. Our paper introduces a system integrating NFTs, IPFS, and smart contracts across various EVM-compatible platforms such as Binance

Smart Chain, Polygon, Fantom, and Celo, focusing on enhancing security, transparency, and efficiency. Unlike Li et al. [9] and Fusco et al. [3], who balance transparency with privacy, our system uses NFTs for voter identification and IPFS for secure data storage. Building on the security focus of Singh et al. [13] and Khan et al. [6], our approach adds a multi-platform deployment strategy and smart contracts, providing a more robust security framework.

In examining decentralization and privacy, our research builds on the foundational work by Patil et al. [11] and Indapwar et al. [5], which emphasizes the decentralized nature of blockchain. Our study extends this by integrating NFTs and IPFS to bolster privacy and security, using NFTs for voter identification and IPFS for secure data storage, thereby enhancing data integrity and maintaining voter anonymity. Comparatively, while Hjalmarsson et al. [4] provide a detailed analysis of blockchain solutions in e-voting, our framework is designed specifically for electoral systems, focusing on practicality and scalability. Kumar et al. [7] explore securing voter details and votes on separate blockchains, whereas our approach employs a unified system with NFTs and IPFS, improving both transparency and security in the electoral process.

3   Approach

3.1   Traditional Model of Management Vote

The traditional election process is defined by a complex network of interactions and responsibilities, which are essential for delivering a fair and representative outcome in a democracy (see Fig. 1 for more details). This model relies on several key elements: the well-informed participation of voters, the practical use of ballots, the secure storage of ballot boxes, careful counting by election officials, and the final announcement of results. Each component works together to maintain the integrity, transparency, and accuracy of the electoral process, ensuring that the will of the people is accurately captured and respected. The detailed functions of these components are outlined below:

Electors: In democratic societies, electors are responsible for participating in elections to select leaders or decide on key issues. Their choices, informed by personal beliefs, mirror the range of opinions within the society and play a fundamental role in its governance.

Ballot: Serving as the primary method for recording votes, the ballot can be a paper document or a digital interface. Its design prioritizes clarity and confidentiality, which are essential for maintaining the integrity of the vote and the privacy of the voter, thereby supporting the exercise of democratic rights.

Ballot Box: The ballot box is a secure receptacle used to collect and safeguard all cast ballots. It is a symbol of the integrity of the voting process, protecting the confidentiality of the votes until they are counted.

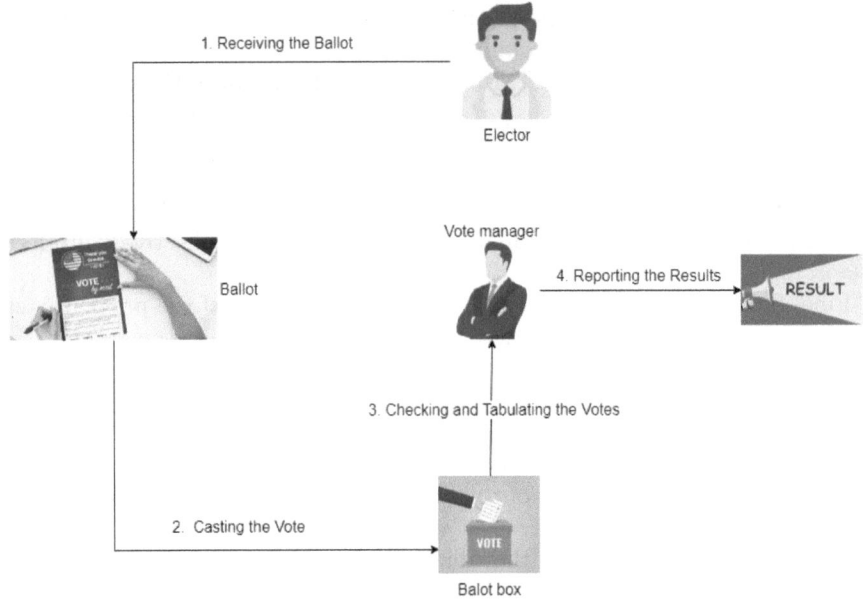

Fig. 1. Traditional model of management vote

Vote Managers: Vote managers ensure the fairness and accuracy of the electoral process. They are tasked with the careful scrutiny and tallying of each ballot, verifying that every vote complies with established regulations and accurately captures the electors' intentions.

Election Results: The final election results, which emerge from the careful tabulation of votes, encapsulate the collective will of the electorate. These results are fundamental in shaping policy, determining leadership, and upholding the principles of democracy.

Step 1: Receiving the Ballot. When voters arrive at their assigned polling stations, their first task is to verify their eligibility to vote by presenting a voter identification card. This card confirms their registered status and their entitlement to vote. Once their eligibility is confirmed, voters are given their ballots. At this point, they are reminded of the seriousness of their civic responsibility. They take time to consider their options, recognizing that each selection on the ballot represents not just a preference for a candidate or policy but also their hopes and concerns for their community and country. This step is crucial as it lays the foundation for a fair and transparent voting process.

Step 2: Casting the Ballot. Inside the privacy of the voting booth, voters mark their ballots, ensuring the confidentiality of their choices-a fundamental aspect of a democratic election. This private act has significant public implications. After making their choices, voters deposit their completed ballots into a secure ballot box, symbolizing their participation in the democratic process and contributing to the collective voice of their community.

Step 3: Counting the Votes. This critical phase begins after the voting period ends. Election officials meticulously inspect each ballot to ensure it adheres to the guidelines and is free from irregularities. This scrutiny is essential for maintaining the legitimacy of the election. The ballots are then counted, either manually or electronically, based on the available technology and established procedures. This step aggregates the individual votes, reflecting the collective will of the electorate.

Final Step: Announcing the Results. The diligent work of the previous steps culminates in this final phase, where election officials compile the vote data to determine the election winners or the outcomes of various issues. The announcement of the results is more than a mere reporting of numbers; it marks the culmination of the democratic process. These results set the direction for future policies, leadership, and governance, directly shaped by the electorate's decisions. The transparency and accuracy of this announcement are critical in maintaining public trust in the democratic process and ensuring that the elected representatives or policies truly represent the will of the people.

3.2 Blockchain-Based Approach for Management Voting Integrating Smart Contract, RSA-Encrypted NFT, IPFS, and Blockchain Techniques

The traditional election process, with its long history, has several drawbacks that can affect its efficiency and reliability. Common issues include the risk of fraud, human errors during vote counting, delays in tabulating results, and concerns regarding voter privacy and ballot security. These problems are often exacerbated by the reliance on physical infrastructure and manual procedures, which can introduce inefficiencies and raise operational costs. As a potential solution, a blockchain-based approach to election management is being considered. This approach utilizes Blockchain technology, Smart Contracts, encrypted Non-Fungible Tokens (NFTs), and the InterPlanetary File System (IPFS) to address these challenges. By applying blockchain, the voting process gains enhanced integrity and transparency through a secure, unalterable ledger. Smart Contracts help automate various voting tasks, minimizing the chances of human error and fraud. RSA encrypted NFTs serve to secure unique voter identities, ensuring one vote per individual while preserving anonymity. Additionally, IPFS provides a decentralized storage option that bolsters data security and improves accessibility. The following sections will delve into more details about these components.

Building on the framework outlined in our previous article [14], we seek to improve transparency in election management by incorporating encrypted Non-Fungible Tokens (NFTs). Our strategy utilizes technologies such as Smart Contracts, encrypted NFTs, the InterPlanetary File System (IPFS), and Blockchain to address the shortcomings of conventional voting systems. Figure 2 depicts the architecture of this method, which includes several components aimed at refining the electoral process. These components comprise a User Interface designed for easy navigation and data entry, a Personal Identification Code to securely identify voters, Smart Contracts to automate and validate electoral tasks, encrypted NFTs to digitalize and authenticate each vote, IPFS for decentralized and robust data storage, and a Distributed Ledger to keep a transparent and unalterable record of all transactions and interactions. This configuration is intended to enhance the precision and integrity of the voting processes, ensuring that every step, from voter registration to the announcement of results, is verifiable and secure.

- **Personal Identification Code** In blockchain-based voting systems, the Personal Identification Code is essential for authenticating voter identities and verifying their eligibility. This code helps to prevent unauthorized access and fraudulent activities, thereby supporting the integrity and fairness of the election process.
- **Electronic Voting Card** The Electronic Voting Card is a digital element within blockchain voting that stores critical voter and candidate information. Integrated into the blockchain and safeguarded by smart contracts and encrypted Non-Fungible Tokens, it ensures secure and immutable management of voter data.
- **User Interface** The User Interface in blockchain-based elections is designed to be user-friendly, allowing voters to easily cast their votes and access pertinent election information. It also provides real-time updates and a transparent view of the electoral process.
- **Vote Manager** In a blockchain voting system, the Vote Manager is tasked with compiling and reporting the election results, ensuring they are accurately and transparently aggregated. This role combines technological expertise with an understanding of electoral practices.
- **Smart Contracts for Transparency in Decision-Making** Smart contracts are crucial for automating key electoral processes, such as vote counting and verifying voter eligibility, thereby increasing transparency and reducing the likelihood of errors or manipulation.
- **Encrypted NFTs** Encrypted Non-Fungible Tokens are used to record each vote as a unique, secure, and unalterable record, enhancing the security and distinctiveness of the voting process.
- **IPFS** The InterPlanetary File System supports the decentralized and efficient distribution of election results, ensuring they are readily available and resistant to censorship, which enhances the accessibility and reliability of the disseminated information.
- **Distributed Ledger** The distributed ledger provides a synchronized and decentralized database that is ideal for maintaining the integrity of election-related data, ensuring that information such as votes, voter registrations, and results are consistently recorded and accessible across various network nodes.

The new blockchain-based election model offers a different approach to managing the voting process, providing notable improvements over traditional methods. This model integrates technologies such as distributed ledgers, smart con-

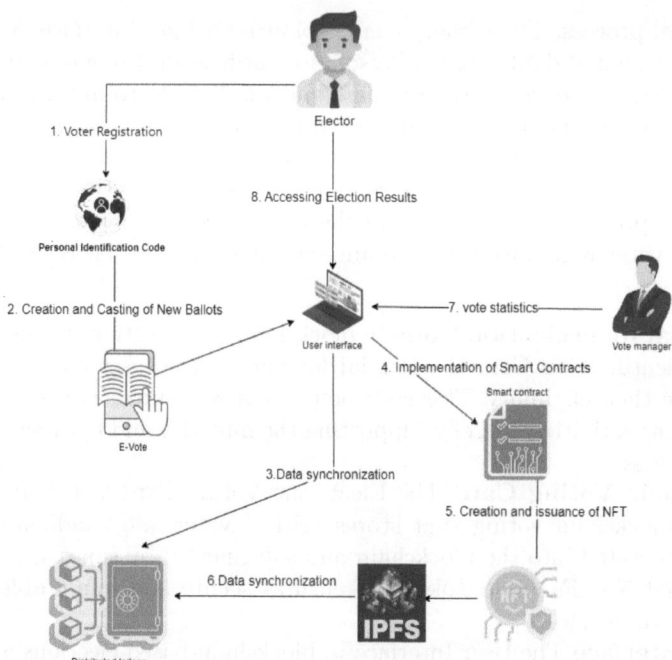

Fig. 2. Blockchain-based model for management voting: Integrating Smart Contract, NFT, IPFS, and Blockchain Techniquese

tracts, and encrypted Non-Fungible Tokens (NFTs), enhancing the security, transparency, and efficiency of elections. The blockchain's immutable ledger records each vote securely, making it resistant to tampering, while smart contracts help to simplify and streamline operations, minimizing the chance for human errors and fraud. Additionally, the use of encrypted NFTs for voter identification and the InterPlanetary File System (IPFS) for data storage strengthens the overall security and integrity of the system. This method improves the accessibility and convenience of the voting process for electors and helps to sustain public confidence in the electoral system, representing a noteworthy development in democratic voting practices (refer to Fig. 2 for more details).

Step 1: Voter Registration. In the initial phase, voters are required to register in the system with their unique personal identification codes. This code is essential for maintaining the privacy and security of personal information while confirming voter eligibility. The registration process aims to create a secure and authenticated voter base, which is fundamental in establishing a reliable electoral process. This step is critical to prevent fraudulent voting and double registrations by ensuring each voter's identity is verified and securely logged in the system.

Step 2: Creation and Casting of New Ballots. Once registered, voters use the system's interface to create their ballots. This step can be performed remotely, increasing the accessibility and convenience of voting. It enables a wider participation, including from those unable to reach traditional polling stations. The ballot creation process is designed to be clear and straightforward, allowing voters to confidently make their selections.

Step 3: Synchronization of Data to the Distributed Ledger. After the ballots are created, details regarding the voters and new ballots are synchronized to a distributed ledger. This ledger acts as an immutable record, maintaining the transparency and integrity of the voting data. This step is vital in preserving the trustworthiness of the electoral process by preventing any changes or tampering with the votes once they are cast.

Step 4: Implementation of Smart Contracts. Smart contracts are utilized to automate various aspects of the electoral process. These contracts manage tasks such as verifying voting rights, confirming ballot validity, and securely recording votes. The implementation of smart contracts streamlines the election, making it more efficient and less susceptible to errors, tampering, or fraud.

Step 5: Encrypted NFT Creation and Storage on IPFS. Validated ballots are converted into encrypted Non-Fungible Tokens (NFTs) and stored on the InterPlanetary File System (IPFS). This step ensures the security and uniqueness of each vote. By using blockchain technology, each vote is preserved as a distinct and unchangeable record, enhancing the security of the electoral process.

Step 6: Re-Synchronization to the Distributed Ledger. Following the creation of encrypted NFTs, details of these tokens are re-synchronized to the distributed ledger. This ensures all election-related data remain consistent and transparent, maintaining a comprehensive and unalterable record from the beginning to the end of the election.

Step 7: Analysis and Evaluation of Election Results. Election administrators then utilize the system interface to perform a statistical analysis and evaluation of the election results. This process, automated using smart contracts, increases the accuracy of the results and reduces the possibility of human error. This step is crucial for providing a clear and accurate interpretation of the electoral outcomes.

Step 8: Accessing Election Results. Finally, voters and other stakeholders can access and review the election results through the system's interface. This step enhances transparency and trust in the electoral process by allowing voters to easily verify the outcomes. It ensures that the results are readily accessible and comprehensible to all interested parties, reinforcing the credibility of the election.

4   Evaluation

4.1   Evaluation of Encrypted NFT Framework for Efficiency in Vaccine Management in Children

In the Evaluation section of our paper, we review various encryption algorithms to ensure the security of metadata for encrypted Non-Fungible Tokens (NFTs), essential components of our blockchain-based election management system. We explore six key encryption methods-RSA, RC4, DES, ChaCha20, Blowfish, and AES-to determine the best balance between security and operational efficiency. This analysis is critical for ensuring the system's effectiveness and reliability. Each algorithm is assessed based on its encryption speed and the level of security it offers, particularly focusing on its ability to safeguard encrypted NFTs and data on the InterPlanetary File System (IPFS). The results include performance metrics for encrypting both text and image data, which are crucial for upholding the integrity and transparency of the voting process. These findings are systematically presented in detailed tables (Table 1).

Table 1. RSA Encryption and Decryption Performance for Image and text Data in Microseconds

RSA	1	2	3	4	5	6	7	8	9	10
Generating key	75356	95235	38750	78216	98703	95067	54002	301008	75905	98625
Encrypting image	10678	9685	8111	9330	9393	10638	11635	10350	10979	10646
Decrypting image	262878	265051	269676	255449	258359	265588	255306	258615	259331	260586
Generating key	109072	161201	58533	54586	24110	94431	168443	31826	46018	82341
Encrypting text	0	0	0	0	1367	0	0	0	0	998
Decrypting text	594	1413	1160	1274	501	1084	1378	1508	502	0

Firstly, we specifically evaluated the performance of RSA, an asymmetric encryption method. Our findings showed that RSA key generation times were highly variable, ranging from 75,356 μs to 301,008 μs in different tests. Moreover, both encryption and decryption times for data pertinent to the voting process were extended, with decryption times often surpassing 250,000 μs. These results indicate that while RSA provides robust security, its slower operational speeds could potentially hinder the computational efficiency, impacting the overall performance of election management systems. This consideration is crucial in maintaining the transparency and reliability of the voting process (Table 2).

Secondly, our findings regarding the RC4 algorithm highlighted its notably quick encryption and decryption times for both image and text data, often occurring nearly instantaneously. This characteristic suggests that RC4 could potentially improve transaction processing speeds within our system. However, RC4's

Table 2. RC4 Encryption and Decryption Performance for Image and text Data in Microseconds

RC4 (image)	1	2	3	4	5	6	7	8	9	10
Encrypting image	107	0	0	0	171	0	543	0	0	0
Decrypting image	0	0	664	0	0	0	0	0	1502	0
Encrypting text	0	0	0	0	0	0	0	0	0	0
Decrypting text	0	0	0	0	0	0	0	0	0	0

security strength is comparatively weaker than more modern encryption methods, prompting concerns about its appropriateness for use in environments where data integrity and security are paramount. This compromise between the high speed of RC4 and its reduced security level might restrict its utility in our system, especially in light of similar challenges identified with the RSA algorithm, where the slower processing speeds could adversely affect system efficiency. These considerations are crucial for ensuring the transparency and reliability of the electoral process (Table 3).

Table 3. DES Encryption and Decryption Performance for Image and text Data in Microseconds

DES (image)	1	2	3	4	5	6	7	8	9	10
Encrypting image	1073	540	820	1047	1091	708	1217	599	1121	1024
Decrypting image	1058	551	0	819	606	999	1005	1018	501	0
Encrypting text	0	0	0	0	0	0	0	0	0	0
Decrypting text	0	0	0	0	0	508	0	0	0	0

Thirdly, we evaluated the DES algorithm, which demonstrated moderate processing speeds. Specifically, encryption times for image data were recorded between 540 and 1,217 µs, with decryption times reaching up to 1,058 µs. These figures suggest that DES could potentially improve the operational efficiency of voting systems through its relatively quick processing times. However, the known security weaknesses of DES introduce substantial concerns. The possibility that data integrity could be undermined by these vulnerabilities indicates that the advantages of faster processing might not outweigh the risks. This issue is reflective of similar challenges faced with other algorithms like RC4 and RSA, where the balance between speed and security presents a significant dilemma in ensuring the transparency and reliability of the electoral process (Table 4).

Forly, ChaCha20 demonstrated a good balance between encryption speed and security. Encrypting image data required only 501 µs, with decryption times also showing efficiency, though with some variability. This level of performance indicates that ChaCha20 could significantly enhance the security of metadata in

Table 4. Chacha20 Encryption and Decryption Performance for Image and text Data in Microseconds

CHACHA20 (image)	1	2	3	4	5	6	7	8	9	10
Encrypting image	501	0	109	0	0	0	0	0	0	101
Decrypting image	0	584	511	0	0	668	0	634	0	0
Encrypting text	0	0	0	0	0	0	0	0	0	0
Decrypting text	0	0	0	0	0	508	0	0	0	0

voting systems due to its quick data processing and robust security attributes. Given the concerns with other encryption algorithms-such as the known vulnerabilities of DES, the significant security issues with RC4, and the slower processing times of RSA-ChaCha20 emerges as a suitable option, especially when the integrity and confidentiality of sensitive election data are paramount. This choice supports the overall goal of maintaining transparency and reliability in electoral systems (Table 5).

Table 5. Blowfish Encryption and Decryption Performance for Image and text Data in Microseconds

blowfish (image)	1	2	3	4	5	6	7	8	9	10
Encrypting image	542	603	506	599	507	1145	608	1137	633	541
Decrypting image	0	0	508	512	501	501	1037	999	575	532
Encrypting text	0	0	537	520	0	533	91	0	0	0
Decrypting text	0	0	0	0	0	0	0	0	0	0

Fifthly, Blowfish demonstrated moderate performance, with encryption times for image data ranging from 506 to 1,145 µs. Traditionally, Blowfish has been appreciated for its reasonable balance of speed and security. Nonetheless, with the emergence of newer encryption technologies that offer enhanced security features, the relevance of Blowfish in contemporary systems might be waning. This prompts concerns about its capability to effectively secure sensitive voting data amidst evolving cybersecurity threats. These concerns are analogous to those identified with DES, which is known for its vulnerabilities, and the compromises between speed and security observed in RC4, RSA, and ChaCha20, underscoring the ongoing challenges in maintaining the integrity and transparency of electoral systems (Table 6).

Finally, AES demonstrated robust performance, achieving encryption times close to zero microseconds and decryption times as low as 504 µs in certain tests. Known for its strong security capabilities, AES ensures consistent and efficient performance, making it a suitable choice for securing sensitive voting data. This level of reliability aligns with our system's requirements for both

Table 6. AES Encryption and Decryption Performance for Image and text Data in Microseconds

AES (image)	1	2	3	4	5	6	7	8	9	10
Encrypting image	0	360	0		82	592	608	502	541	510	513
Decrypting image	1332	0		1005	0	504	0	0	0	0	0
Encrypting text	0	0	0		0	0	0	0	507	0	0
Decrypting text	0	0	0		0	0	0	0	0	0	0

protecting electoral information and ensuring rapid data accessibility. Similar challenges and considerations have been observed with other algorithms such as Blowfish, ChaCha20, and DES, which also focus on maintaining data integrity and adapting to evolving cybersecurity threats.

The data we have gathered provides insights into the performance of various encryption algorithms for managing data within a blockchain-based voting system. We are evaluating six encryption methods-RSA, RC4, DES, ChaCha20, Blowfish, and AES-to find the right balance between security and operational efficiency. Our system, which utilizes smart contracts and encrypted NFTs to secure and manage voting records, needs an encryption strategy that can handle the dynamic and diverse nature of electoral transactions. Our extensive testing and analysis aim to select an encryption method that meets strict security standards while facilitating the rapid operational pace essential for efficient management of voting information. This approach is crucial for maintaining a reliable and transparent system that election authorities and voters can trust.

4.2 Testing on EVM-Supported Platforms

In our analysis of blockchain technology's role in enhancing the transparency of voting systems, this paper examines the integration of Blockchain, encrypted NFTs, and IPFS to ensure the traceability and authenticity of voting records. We focus on three key functions within this framework: data creation, NFT minting, and NFT transfer, which are critical for recording, verifying, and securely exchanging voting data across electoral systems.

We evaluate four Ethereum Virtual Machine (EVM)-compatible blockchain platforms-BNB Chain (formerly known as Binance Smart Chain), Fantom, Celo, and Polygon-each chosen for its unique capabilities in supporting these functions. Our analysis considers the transaction fees and operational efficiencies of each platform to assess their suitability for electoral applications.

- BNB Chain offers high throughput and low transaction costs, beneficial for applications that demand scalability and efficiency. It is designed to support decentralized applications (dApps) and NFT transactions effectively.
- Fantom excels in security, scalability, and decentralization, featuring a unique consensus mechanism that provides near-instant transaction finality-key for electoral systems requiring timely and reliable data updates.

Table 7. Transaction fee

	Transaction Creation	Create NFT	Transfer NFT
BNB	0.0273134 BNB ($16.47)	0.00109162 BNB ($0.66)	0.00057003 BNB ($0.34)
Fantom	0.00957754 FTM ($0.00)	0.000405167 FTM ($0.00)	0.0002380105 FTM ($0.00)
Polygon	0.006840710032835408 MATIC ($0.01)	0.000289405001852192 MATIC ($0.00)	0.000170007501088048 MATIC ($0.00)
Celo	0.007097844 CELO ($0.005)	0.0002840812 CELO ($0.000)	0.0001554878 CELO ($0.000)

- Celo is designed with a mobile-first approach, enhancing blockchain accessibility among smartphone users, which is vital for voting management in regions with limited access to conventional computing resources. Its emphasis on accessibility and low fees aims to create a more inclusive voting system.
- Polygon provides multi-chain scalability solutions that support rapid and cost-effective transactions, making it suitable for managing complex operations such as NFT minting and transfer.

Our objective is to deliver a thorough analysis of these platforms' effectiveness in creating a secure and efficient system for managing voting transparency. By reviewing the transaction fees for data creation, NFT minting, and NFT transfer, we provide insights into the economic feasibility of these technologies in electoral contexts. This analysis is grounded in a realistic evaluation of each platform's strengths and limitations, offering a clear perspective on the potential and challenges of integrating blockchain technology into electoral management.

Transaction Fee Analysis: Table 7 compares transaction fees on Binance Smart Chain (BNB), Fantom (FTM), Polygon (MATIC), and Celo (CELO) for a framework enhancing voting management using encrypted NFTs and smart contracts. These platforms are chosen for their compatibility with the Ethereum Virtual Machine (EVM), crucial for implementing our smart contracts. The table also indicates the token market values for these platforms as of May 27, 2024, at 7:00:00 AM UTC, providing an economic context for adopting these blockchain technologies in the voting system.

Firstly, Binance Smart Chain lists transaction fees at 0.0273134 BNB ($16.47), minting an NFT at 0.00109162 BNB ($0.66), and transferring an NFT at 0.00057003 BNB ($0.34). These fees suggest that Binance Smart Chain is a robust platform, though potentially more expensive than alternatives. Secondly, Fantom offers a more affordable solution, with the cost for executing a new transaction at 0.00957754 FTM, a nominal dollar amount. Fees for NFT creation and transfer on Fantom are 0.000405167 FTM and 0.0002380105 FTM, respectively, both translating to minimal dollar values, positioning it as a cost-effective choice for transaction management. Thirdly, Polygon records the fee for starting a transaction at 0.006840710032835408 MATIC, or just $0.01. Creating an NFT on Polygon costs 0.000289405001852192 MATIC, and transferring an NFT costs 0.000170007501088048 MATIC. Both expenses are negligible, indicating minimal financial impact for operations on this platform. Finally, Celo charges 0.007097844 CELO for initiating a transaction, about $0.005. Fees for NFT creation and transfer are 0.0002840812 CELO and 0.0001554878 CELO, respectively, both under a cent, making Celo an economically viable option for managing transactions.

Together, the data in Table 7 provides a comparative overview of the transaction costs across different blockchain platforms, crucial for stakeholders considering the integration of blockchain technology into voting management. It is essential for stakeholders to consider these costs carefully, as they directly affect the financial viability of adopting blockchain solutions. Each platform offers a distinct cost profile that should be evaluated based on the specific needs and operational scope they are intended to support within the voting management system.

5 Conclusion

Our investigation confirms that the integration of blockchain technology, smart contracts, encrypted NFTs, and IPFS can significantly improve the management of voting systems. The decentralized nature of blockchain provides enhanced security and transparency, critical for maintaining the integrity and trust in democratic processes. The use of smart contracts and encrypted NFTs further aids in ensuring that only authorized entities access voting records, thereby upholding voter privacy and data security. Performance evaluations across multiple blockchain platforms have demonstrated the system's operational effectiveness and highlighted considerations for cost efficiency. Ultimately, this study underscores the viability of blockchain technologies in evolving and modernizing electoral systems, providing a framework that supports the security, transparency, and efficiency needs of voting management.

References

1. Elklit, J., Reynolds, A.: The impact of election administration on the legitimacy of emerging democracies: a new comparative politics research agenda. Commonwealth Comp. Politics 40(2), 86–119 (2002)
2. Ferreira, L., Cruz, M.R., Cruz, E.F., Quintela, H., Cunha, M.C.: Supporting Technologies and the Impact of Blockchain on Organizations and Society. IGI Global (2023)
3. Fusco, F., Lunesu, M.I., Pani, F.E., Pinna, A.: Crypto-voting, a blockchain based e-voting system. In: KMIS, pp. 221–225 (2018)
4. Hjálmarsson, F.Þ., Hreiarsson, G.K., Hamdaqa, M., Hjálmtýsson, G.: Blockchain-based e-voting system. In: 2018 IEEE 11th International Conference on Cloud Computing (CLOUD), pp. 983–986. IEEE (2018)

5. Indapwar, A., Chandak, M., Jain, A.: E-voting system using blockchain technology. Int. J. Adv. Trends Comput. Sci. Eng. **9**(3) 2775–2779 (2020)
6. Khan, K.M., Arshad, J., Khan, M.M.: Secure digital voting system based on blockchain technology. Int. J. Electron. Gov. Res. (IJEGR) **14**(1), 53–62 (2018)
7. Kumar, D.D., Chandini, D., Reddy, D., Bhattacharyya, D., Kim, T.: Secure electronic voting system using blockchain technology. Int. J. Smart Home **14**(2), 31–38 (2020)
8. Le, N.T.T., et al.: Assuring non-fraudulent transactions in cash on delivery by introducing double smart contracts. Int. J. Adv. Comput. Sci. Appl. **10**(5), 677–684 (2019)
9. Li, C., Xiao, J., Dai, X., Jin, H.: AMVchain: authority management mechanism on blockchain-based voting systems. Peer-to-peer Netw. Appl. **14**, 2801–2812 (2021)
10. Moynihan, D.P.: Building secure elections: e-voting, security, and systems theory. Public Adm. Rev. **64**(5), 515–528 (2004)
11. Patil, H.V., Rathi, K.G., Tribhuwan, M.V.: A study on decentralized e-voting system using blockchain technology. Int. Res. J. Eng. Technol **5**(11), 48–53 (2018)
12. Quoc, K.L., et al.: SSSB: an approach to insurance for cross-border exchange by using smart contracts. In: Awan, I., Younas, M., Poniszewska-Marańda, A. (eds.) Mobile Web and Intelligent Information Systems. MobiWIS 2022. LNCS, vol. 13475, pp. 179–192. Springer, Cham (2022). https://doi.org/10.1007/978-3-031-14391-5_14
13. Singh, A., Chatterjee, K.: SecEVS: secure electronic voting system using blockchain technology. In: 2018 International Conference on Computing, Power and Communication Technologies (GUCON), pp. 863–867. IEEE (2018)
14. Trong, N.D.P., et al.: Blockchain-enhanced pediatric vaccine management: a novel approach integrating NFTs, IPFS, and smart contracts. In: Luo, M., Zhang, LJ. (eds.) Services Computing - SCC 2023. SCC 2023. LNCS, vol. 14211, pp. 63–78. Springer, Cham (2024). https://doi.org/10.1007/978-3-031-51674-0_5
15. Weir, K.: Safeguarding democracy: increasing election integrity through enhanced voter verification. Homeland Security Affairs (2018)

A Vehicular Network Routing Based on the DQN Algorithm in the Cloud Environment

Mingzhu Ge[1], Liya Xu[2(✉)] ⓘ, Junhui Wang[1], Caicai Zhang[3], Jiaoli Shi[2], and Hongbo Li[4]

[1] Taizhou Vocational College of Science and Technology, Taizhou 318020, Zhejiang, China
[2] Jiujiang University, Jiujiang 332005, Jiangxi, China
xuliya603@whu.edu.cn
[3] Zhejiang Polytechnic University of Mechanical and Electrical Engineering, Hangzhou 310000, Zhejiang, China
[4] Daqing Normal University, Daqing 163712, Heilongjiang, China

Abstract. The Internet of Vehicles (IoVs), composed of smart cars, roadside nodes, base stations, and the like, has emerged as one of the most prevailing research fields. The IoVs constitutes a delay-sensitive context that requires low-delay services; yet, the current quality of routing services is unassured. The cloud-edge collaboration solution possesses powerful computing and storage capabilities along with relatively short transmission latency, and can fulfill the diverse requirements of users to the maximum extent. This paper conducts research on the routing problem within the IoVs assisted by cloud-edge collaboration to further reduce the service delay of the IoVs. This paper presents a vehicular network routing scheme based on the DQN algorithm. The service nodes make routing decisions and content caching decisions for each request by the user request information and the current network resource status within the system. The proposed strategy attains the goal of reducing network latency and improving service quality by jointly optimizing the allocation of computing, caching, and communication resources. Simulation results indicate that the proposed strategy performs better than the existing cloud-edge collaboration solutions and converges rapidly in network environments with diverse parameters.

Keywords: IoVs · Routing · Cloud Computing

1 Introduction

The rapid progress of wireless communication technologies and the extensive utilization of mobile intelligent terminals have enabled high-speed interconnection between devices and networks as well as among devices themselves. Simultaneously, to enhance the transportation efficiency and safety of vehicles, there is an acute need to develop more reliable and efficient vehicle interconnection systems [1]. As a novel paradigm, the IoVs, underpinned by the ubiquitous sensing capabilities of the IoT, connects vehicles to the Internet. The IoVs is capable of promptly exchanging vehicle information through the network

Y. Wang and L.-J. Zhang (Eds.): CLOUD 2024, LNCS 15423, pp. 37–45, 2025.
https://doi.org/10.1007/978-3-031-77153-8_4

and providing efficient and low-delay transportation services. Nevertheless, tasks with high computing complexity, large data volumes, frequent collaborative communication among vehicles, and limited spectrum bandwidth pose formidable challenges to offering delay-sensitive IoVs services. Consequently, ensuring low-delay communication within the IoVs has emerged as a significant predicament.

Initially, cloud computing, furnished with its vigorous computing and storage capabilities [2, 3], emerged as the primary solution for the IoVs, being employed to handle an abundance of highly complex computing tasks within the IoVs and transmit copious amounts of data to vehicles. However, due to privacy protection issues in the cloud [4, 5] and the considerable transmission distance between the cloud and vehicles, it gives rise to a significant transmission delay between them, making it challenging to meet the low-delay requirements of the IoVs system. To accomplish real-time communication and decision-making, researchers embarked on considering the application of edge computing in the IoVs scenario. Edge computing is capable of alleviating the computing and transmission delay in the IoVs by processing requests from vehicles in Road Side Unite (RSU) and Base Station (BS).

However, the computing and communication capabilities of edge computing are constrained, which prompts scholars to contemplate the synergy between the cloud and the edge [6]. The cloud-edge collaboration architecture can not only handle large-scale computing tasks in the IoVs but also enable real-time interaction with vehicles, substantively enhancing the service quality of the IoVs and reducing the service delay [7, 8]. To further reduce the delay of the IoVs, scholars have conducted research on task partitioning within the IoVs assisted by cloud-edge collaboration. By partitioning and offloading tasks to RSU, BS, or cloud servers for parallel or sequential execution in a more meticulous and rational manner, the computing and storage resources of local devices, the edge, and cloud servers can be fully exploited to further optimize the delay of the IoVs. Considering the advantages of Deep Q Network in data processing and analysis as well as decision-making, its application in the IoVs system assisted by cloud-edge collaboration can enhance network performance by implementing intelligent and judicious resource allocation. Although the existing IoVs data transmission schemes based on cloud-edge collaboration can optimize service delay and reliability by partitioning tasks and optimizing resource allocation, to a considerable extent, they overlook the impact of network cross-layer collaborative caching and routing, as well as the influence resulting from network heterogeneity.

Consequently, this paper proposes a novel routing mechanism based on the DQN algorithm, which makes cross-layer collaborative caching and routing decisions for the arriving requests in line with the user's request information and the currently available network resources in the system. Simulations based on a considerable amount of real data suggest that the strategy proposed in this paper demonstrates superior performance compared to the existing cloud-edge collaboration solutions and converges rapidly in various scenarios.

2 System Model

2.1 Network Model

In this section, the topological structure of the network is initially introduced based on the connection of RSU and BS in the heterogeneous network and the manner in which vehicle terminals access the base station. For the purpose of effectively analyzing the delay problem of the IoVs, Fig. 1 presents the structural schematic diagram of the network model. In a top-down sequence, the uppermost layer is the cloud, encompassing one or more cloud servers; the middle layer is BS, and the layer nearest to the vehicles is RSU. Each RSU or BS possesses the capabilities of caching and computing, and the access requests of vehicle terminals can be fulfilled by RSU, BS or the cloud. The cloud stores the target content and resources requested by all users, while the caching and computing capabilities of RSU and BS are limited. Hence, comprehensively considering the joint allocation of caching, computing and communication resources in the hierarchical heterogeneous IoVs involving vehicle terminals, RSU, BS and cloud servers can reduce the processing delay time of access requests and the transmission efficiency of target content in the vehicle network, and enhance the quality of user services.

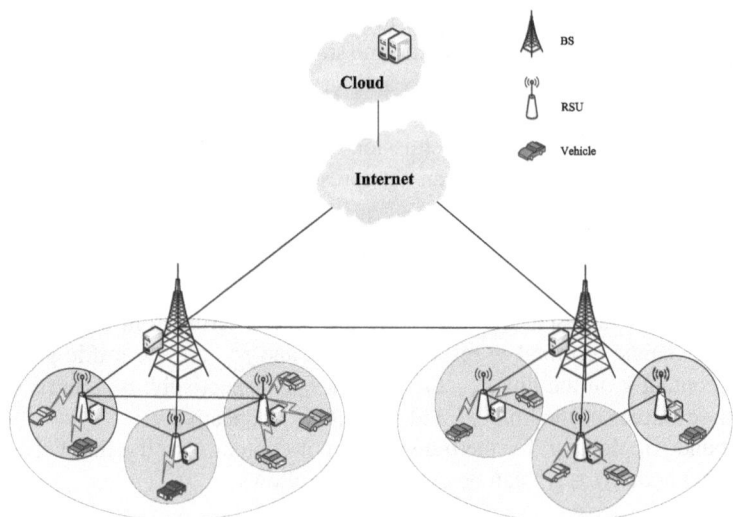

Fig. 1. Network model of the IoVs with cloud-edge cooperation

The network model of the multi-layer heterogeneous IoVs featuring cloud-edge collaboration can be depicted as a directed graph $G(N, L)$, wherein N and L constitute the aggregations of nodes and physical links within the network model. The physical link between node p and node j can be denoted as $L_{p,j}$. N serves as the collective term for the sets of RSU, BS, and cloud servers, respectively represented by N_R, N_B and N_C. Due to the restricted caching capacity of RSU and BS, all contents are cached in the initial state of the cloud server. When a vehicle terminal transmits an access request (attempting to obtain the target content), it initially dispatches the corresponding access request to the accessed RSU. If the target content is currently cached in the RSU, the RSU will convey the target content to the vehicle terminal; otherwise, the access request will be routed to the directly connected RSU of the current RSU node, the attached BS, and its directly connected BS for sequential processing. If none of the aforementioned nodes can satisfy the access request from the vehicle terminal, the cloud will transfer the target content to the vehicle terminal.

2.2 Delay Model

The total delay for vehicle terminals to obtain the target content comprises the transmission delay on the physical links and the carry delay on the nodes (RSU, BS, and cloud servers). These two types of delays can be modeled independently and then aggregated to acquire the total delay, thereby establishing the delay optimization model based on the total delay. For the i-th RSU, A_i is the set of its directly connected RSUs, and the set of directly connected vehicles can be expressed as M_i, and the directly connected BS is designated as B_i. Similarly, A_{B_i} is the set of adjacent BSs of node Bi in the same layer. X_i^k and $X_{B_i}^k$ are two Boolean variables, respectively denoting whether the i-th RSU and the B_i-th BS cache content k. If so, the value is 1; otherwise, they are set to 0.

Transmission Delay Model. Owing to the distinct types of links utilized for content transmission in the IoVs network, the transmission delay can be classified into the transmission delay between vehicle terminals and service nodes, as well as the transmission delay among service nodes.

The round-trip delay for the transmission of content k between the mobile vehicle m and the accessed RSU $i(i \in N_R)$ can be represented as:

$$T_{m,i}^{tr,k} = \frac{f_{m,i}^k}{b_{m,i}} + \frac{f_{i,m}^k}{b_{i,m}} \tag{1}$$

where $l_{m,i}$ and $l_{i,m}$ represent the links from the vehicle terminal m to RSUi and from RSUi to the vehicle terminal m respectively; $f_{m,i}^k$ and $f_{i,m}^k$ are the traffic generated by the target content k on the link $l_{m,i}$ and the link $l_{i,m}$ respectively; $b_{m,i}$ and $b_{i,m}$ are the bandwidth resources of the link $l_{m,i}$ and the link $l_{i,m}$ respectively.

The round-trip delay T for the transmission of content k on the link between node $p(p \in N)$ and node $j(j \in N)$ can be expressed as follows.

$$T_{p,j}^{tr,k} = \frac{f_{p,j}^k}{b_{p,j}} + \frac{f_{j,p}^k}{b_{j,p}} \tag{2}$$

where $l_{p,j}$ and $l_{j,p}$ respectively represent the link from service node p to service node j and the link from service node j to service node $p; f_{p,j}^k$ and $f_{j,p}^k$ respectively indicate the traffic generated by content k on the link $l_{p,j}$ and the link $l_{j,p}; b_{p,j}$ and $b_{j,p}$ respectively denote the bandwidth of the link $l_{p,j}$ and the link $l_{j,p}$.

Carry Delay Model. The carry delay in the IoVs refers to the period from the moment the content of an access request enters a node to the moment it leaves the node, encompassing queuing, service, and processing delays. When an access request arrives at a node, it initially enters the waiting queue and is subsequently processed. The queuing time is induced by the waiting of the request in the queue and is dependent on the service rate of the node and the arrival rate of the requests. The queuing process of user requests at IoVs nodes adheres to the *M/M/k* queuing theory model [9]. The resource utilization rate of node p can be represented as:

$$\rho_p = \frac{\lambda_p}{k_{p,s}\mu_p} \tag{3}$$

Here, ρ_p is the resource utilization rate of node p, λ_p and $k_{p,s}$ respectively denote the request arrival rate and the total number of servers at node p; μ_p represents the service rate of each server at node p, which is predominantly influenced by the operating speed of the CPU and the number of CPU cycles required for the content request.

According to [9], the equilibrium equation of the request queuing system of the network node p in a stable state is as follows.

$$\begin{cases} \lambda_p P_{p,n-1} = n\mu_p P_{p,n}, \, (1 \leq n \leq k_{p,s}) \\ \lambda_p P_{p,n-1} = k_{p,s}\mu_p P_{p,n}, \, (k_{p,s} \leq n) \end{cases} \tag{4}$$

where $P_{p,n}$ represents the probability that there are n access requests in the queuing system of node p.

According to the equation $\sum_{n=0}^{\infty} P_{p,n} = 1$ and $\rho_p == \frac{\lambda_p}{k_{p,s}\mu_p}$, the stable probability of zero requests in node p is denoted as $P_{p,0}$, and the specific formula is

$$P_{p,0} = \left[\sum_{n=0}^{k_{p,s}-1} \frac{(k_{p,s}\rho_p)^n}{n!} + \frac{(k_{p,s}\rho_p)^{k_{p,s}}}{(1-\rho)k_{p,s}!} \right]^{-1} \tag{5}$$

The formula for the stable probability $P_{p,0}$ of there being n access requests in node p is

$$P_{p,n} = \begin{cases} \frac{1}{n!}(k_{p,s}\rho_p)^n P_{p,0}, \, (0 < n \leq k_{p,s}) \\ \frac{k_{p,s}^{k_{p,s}}}{k_{p,s}!}\rho_p^n P_{p,0}, \, (n > k_{p,s}) \end{cases} \tag{6}$$

When all servers of node p are occupied, the access requests that arrive must be queued. At this point, the probability $P_{i,Q}$ that the number of tasks in node p reaches the upper limit of its queue capacity can be calculated by the following formula

$$P_{p,Q} = \sum_{n=k_{p,s}}^{\infty} P_{p,n} = P_{p,0}\frac{k_{p,s}^{k_{p,s}}}{k_{p,s}!}\frac{\rho_p^{k_{p,s}}}{1-\rho_p} \tag{7}$$

Then the total number of access requests in the queue system of node p can be expressed as:

$$N_{p,Q} = P_{p,Q}\frac{\rho_p}{1-\rho_p} \tag{8}$$

In summary, the queuing delay of the access request of the target content k in node p can be expressed as:

$$T_p^q = \frac{N_{p,Q}}{\lambda_p} = \frac{\rho_p}{\lambda_p(1 - \rho_p)}P_{p,Q} \tag{9}$$

The service delay of the access request for the target content in the queue system refers to the delay of obtaining the interested content of the vehicle-mounted device in RSU, BS or the cloud. Therefore, the average service delay of the access request for the target content k in node p can be expressed as $T_p^s = \frac{1}{\mu_p}$.

Adding the queuing delay T_p^q and the service delay T_p^s of the target content k in node p, the carry delay T_p^d of the target content k in node p is obtained. The specific calculation formula is:

$$T_p^d = T_p^q + T_p^s = \frac{\rho_p}{\lambda_p(1 - \rho_p)}P_{p,Q} + \frac{1}{\mu_p} \tag{10}$$

3 Routing Decision Algorithm Based on DQN

The cloud-edge collaborative assisted IoVs constitutes a heterogeneous and dynamic network environment. Traditional algorithms encounter difficulties in formulating rational resource optimization algorithms for such a dynamic and mutable environment. Reinforcement learning is capable of learning the characteristics of the environment through frequent interactions, even in an unfamiliar setting, continuously acquiring experience, and utilizing the feedback signals of the environment to optimize decision-making, thereby enhancing the perception ability within the complex IoVs environment.

In this section, a cross-layer collaborative caching and routing scheme based on DQN is put forward to enhance the resource utilization rate in the IoVs and thereby reduce the system delay. Caching and routing decisions are made based on the historical request information in the IoVs system and the currently available network resources, and a reward function is designed based on the system delay to gradually optimize the parameters of the neural network to improve the cache hit rate of nodes and the routing efficiency of user requests, thereby effectively addressing the delay optimization problem. The following offers detailed introductions to these three elements.

State: The state can be expressed as a set, consisting of caching decisions, the network topology structure, and user request information, and is represented as $s_{p,t} = \{X_{p,s}, \Gamma_t, R_{p,s}, \forall p \in N\}, X_{p,t} = \{X_{p,t}^1, ..., X_{p,t}^k, ..., X_{p,t}^F, \forall k \in K\}$, which is the caching decision vector of each target content on node p in the network model; among them, $X_{p,t}$ is the caching decision of node p for the target content k in the current time slot t. $X_{p,t} = 1$ indicates that node p has cached the content k, and $X_{p,t} = 0$ indicates that the target content k is not cached on the node. Γ_t represents the network topology of the network model in the current time slot t.

$R_{p,t} = \{R_{p,t}^1, ..., R_{p,t}^k, ..., R_{p,t}^F, \forall k \in K\}$ is the user request vector carried on node p in the current time slot t, and $R_{p,t}^k$ represents whether there is a request for the target content k on node p in the current time slot t.

Action: The actions of this algorithm encompass caching decisions and routing decisions, which can be expressed as the set $a_{p,t} = \{X_{p,t+1}, n_{p,t+1}, \forall p \in N\}$, $n_{p,t+1} = \{n^1_{p,t+1}, ..., n^k_{p,t+1}, ..., n^F_{p,t+1}\}$, $k \in K$ representing the routing decision of node p for user requests in the $t + 1$ time slot, and $X_{p,t+1}$ represents the caching decision of node p for the target content k in the $t + 1$ time slot.

Reward: The reward value is a function inversely proportional to the delay, aiming to minimize the system delay through training. The reward obtained by node p in time slot t can be expressed as: $r_{p,t} = \sum_{t=1}^{T_{ep}} \frac{\gamma^{T_{ep}-t}}{T_{m,p}}, \forall p \in N$, T_{ep} is the number of iterative training periods of the DQN model, and γ is the reward discount factor of the DQN model, which can represent the extent of influence of the rewards of historical training periods on the reward value of the current period; $T_{p,t}$ is the sum of the content transmission delay and carry delay between the vehicle terminal m and the service node p in the IoVs network model in time slot t.

4   Simulation Analysis

The topology structure employed for the simulation is a three-layer cloud-edge collaborative assisted network topology. There are F kinds of contents in the network, and the increase in the types of contents results in a decrease in the cache hit rate. The cache size is defined as the relative ratio of the number of contents that a node can cache to F. Given the limited storage capacity of edge devices in real networks, the cache size in the IoVs system ranges from 0.1% to 1% [10]. In the simulation, the "DQN" method proposed in this paper is compared with the existing three solutions in the cloud-edge collaborative IoVs environment to demonstrate the advantages of the proposed solution. These three solutions are "LRU", and "No Cache" [11].

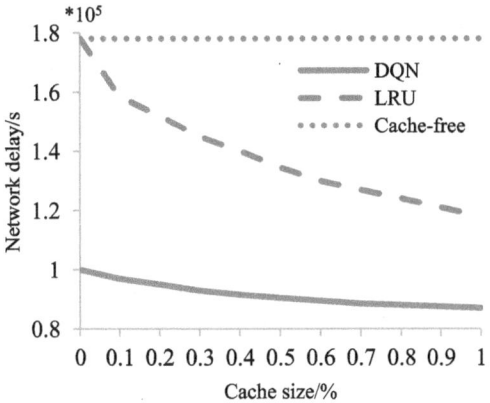

Fig. 2. Network delay of three solutions under different cache sizes

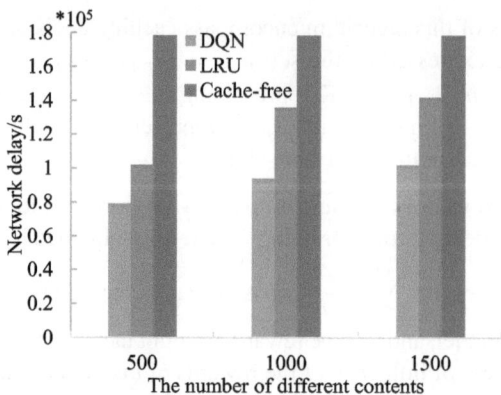

Fig. 3. Network delay of the three solutions when the number of different contents

Figure 2 depicts the network delay of the three schemes under different cache sizes. As illustrated in Fig. 2, when the cache capacity of RSU and BS increases, more popular contents are stored in the network, which significantly reduces the network delay of the solutions with cache. Nevertheless, due to the timely and intelligent caching and routing decisions in the system, the performance of the proposed "DQN" model is far superior to that of other solutions. As the cache size grows, the performance gap brought about by different cache strategies becomes smaller and smaller. Regarding "No Cache", its performance remains unchanged because all requests are routed to the cloud to obtain the content that end users are interested in.

Figure 3 presents the network delay of the three methods when the number of different contents varies. With the increase in the number of different contents, it can be observed from Fig. 3 that the performance of the solutions with cache deteriorates, and the performance gap among them enlarges. The growth of the number of different contents in the network leads to a reduction in the number of requests for popular content by users, which decreases the cache hit rate and increases the network delay. Based on information such as user requests, available resources, and cached contents, the proposed "DQN" model can always make intelligent caching and routing decisions to adapt to changes in the network environment and user preferences, making its performance much better than other schemes. In "No Cache", each request is routed to the cloud to obtain data, keeping its performance invariant.

5 Summary

This paper researches the resource allocation issue in cloud-edge collaborative assisted IoVs. Through the joint optimization of the allocation of computing, caching, and communication resources, the network delay can be reduced and the service quality enhanced. This paper presents a vehicular network routing scheme based on the DQN algorithm. The service nodes make routing decisions and content caching decisions for each request by the user request information and the current network resource status within the system. Simulation results indicate that the strategy proposed in this paper exhibits better performance than the existing cloud-edge collaboration solutions.

Acknowledgment. This work is supported by the National Science Foundation of China (No. 62341206, 62062045), Zhejiang Province Visiting Engineer Cooperation Project (No. FG2023061), Natural Science Fund of Heilongjiang Province in 2022 (No. LH2022G001).

References

1. Qureshi, K.N., Din, S., Jeon, G., Piccialli, F.: Internet of vehicles: key technologies, network model, solutions and challenges with future aspects. IEEE Trans. Intell. Transp. Syst. **22**(3), 1777–1786 (2021)
2. Mei, Z., et al.: Secure multi-dimensional data retrieval with access control and range query in the cloud. Inf. Syst. **122**, 102343 (2024)
3. Feng, J., Yang, L.T., Zhu, Q., Choo, K.K.R.: Privacy-preserving tensor decomposition over encrypted data in a federated cloud environment. IEEE Trans. Dependable Secur. Comput **17**, 857–868 (2018)
4. Yao, S., Ralph, V.J.D., In-Ho, R., Xu, L., Mei, Z., Shi, J.: An identity-based proxy re-encryption scheme with single-hop conditional delegation and multi-hop ciphertext evolution for secure cloud data sharing. IEEE Trans. Inf. Forens. Secur. **18**, 3833–3848 (2023)
5. Wu, Z., Shen, S., Zhou, H., Li, H., Lu, C.: A basic framework for privacy protection in personalized information retrieval. J. Organiz. End User Comput. **33**(6), 1–26 (2021)
6. Feng, J., Yang, L.T., Zhang, R., Qiang, W., Chen, J.: Privacy preserving high-order bi-lanczos in cloud-fog computing for industrial applications. IEEE Trans. Ind. Inform **18**, 7009–7018 (2020)
7. Sharma, S., Kaushik, B.: A survey on internet of vehicles: applications, security issues & solutions. Vehicul. Commun. **20**, 100182 (2019)
8. Feng, M., Krunz, M., Zhang, W.: Joint task partitioning and user association for latency minimization in mobile edge computing networks. IEEE Trans. Veh. Technol. **70**(8), 8108–8121 (2021)
9. Prados-Garzon, J., Ameigeiras, P., Ramos-Munoz, J.J., Navarro-Ortiz, J., Andres-Maldonado, P., Lopez-Soler, M.J.: Performance modeling of softwarized network services based on queuing theory with experimental validation. IEEE Trans. Mob. Comput. **20**(4), 1558–1573 (2021)
10. Li, J., Liu, B., Wu, H.: Energy-efficient in-network caching for content-centric networking. IEEE Commun. Lett. **17**(4), 797–800 (2013)
11. Fang, C., et al.: Deep reinforcement learning based resource allocation for content distribution in fog radio access networks. IEEE Internet Things J. **9**(8), 16874–16883 (2022)

Privacy Preserving Adjacency Query Supporting Homoionym Search over Medical Graph Data in Cloud Computing

Hourong Li[1], Yun Tian[1], Bin Wu[1,2(✉)], and Jiaoli Shi[1,2]

[1] School of Computer and Big Data Science,Jiujiang University,
Jiujiang 332005, China
[2] Jiujiang Key Laboratory of Network and Information Security,
Jiujiang 332005, China
wubcst@163.com

Abstract. Cloud computing is widely used in all walks of life today. Massive amounts of medical graph data are being outsourced to cloud servers to reduce overhead. The untrustworthiness of cloud servers puts the sensitive information of outsourced graph data at risk. To eliminate this security risk, it is an effective method to encrypt sensitive data. The adjacent queries are frequently used and highly valuable in graph data operations, and the adjacency query supporting homoionym search will enlarge the query effect and improve the query function. When the medical graph data is encrypted and stored on the cloud server, the operation of the data becomes extremely difficult. In this article, we propose a scheme to implement the adjacency query supporting homoionym search in cloud computing (AQHS), which maintains search contents privacy. We use a stem extraction algorithm and the searchable encryption mechanism to build secure index, and then achieve the adjacency query. The security of our proposed scheme is verified by formal analysis, and the effectiveness of the scheme is verified by experimental analysis.

Keywords: graph data · adjacency query · searchable encryption · cloud computing

1 Introduction

Cloud computing is widely used in all walks of life today, and it is also accompanied by the popularity of data cloud outsourcing services [1]. The scale of medical graph data is increasing day by day, and the importance and sensitivity of data are important considerations [2]. Due to the unreliability and malicious attacks of cloud servers, these graph data need to be encrypted before outsourcing to cloud servers [3]. In the case of encrypted graph data, it is a very useful operation to achieve the adjacency query supporting homoionym search.

ⓒ The Author(s), under exclusive license to Springer Nature Switzerland AG 2025
Y. Wang and L.-J. Zhang (Eds.): CLOUD 2024, LNCS 15423, pp. 46–55, 2025.
https://doi.org/10.1007/978-3-031-77153-8_5

The adjacency query is a very commonly used operation, and it is often used in the processing of medical graph data and is a fundamental primitive for other operations [4,5]. The community finding, subgraph query and pattern matching are all implemented based on the adjacency queries [6–8]. The adjacency query supporting homoionym search can get more approximate query results, and users can have more choices. We adopt the stem extraction algorithm and searchable encryption mechanism to achieve the adjacency query supporting homoionym search over the outsourcing graph data.

Consider the cost saving reasons, it is necessary to implement this adjacency query directly on the cloud server. At the same time, it is necessary to consider the security of sensitive information. Therefore, achieving this goal in cloud environment is a challenging task [9,10]. For query issues on cloud outsourcing data, the searchable encryption [11–15] is an effective method that allows query work to be directly implemented on cloud servers. At present, the problem of privacy preserving queries on outsourced data is an important research area [16–19]. In the query scenario of cloud outsourcing, a lot of studies have proposed many achievements [20–22]. These existing solutions cannot solve this problem of the adjacency query supporting homoionym search over the encrypted graph data in cloud computing.

To address this issue, we propose a scheme to perform the adjacency query supporting homoionym search over the encrypted graph data in cloud computing (AQHS). The AQHS scheme can achieve adjacency query through an index. We first construct the secure index based on the searchable encryption mechanism and the stem extraction algorithm, then we store the index and encrypted graph data on the cloud server. The cloud server executes the query through the secure index and the user's query request, and returns the query results. The security analysis and the experimental results indicate that the scheme is provably secure and effective. The contribution of the article is summarized as follows.

(1) We propose a scheme to solve the problem of the adjacency query supporting homoionym search over encrypted graph.

(2) We analyze our scheme from the perspective of security to ensure the security of query results.

(3) The experimental analysis results demonstrate the effectiveness of our scheme.

The rest of the article is organized as follows. Section 2 introduces the preliminaries of the article. Section 3 provides the scheme designing. Section 4 and Sect. 5 evaluate our scheme both from security and experiments. Section 6 summarizes the related work. Finally, Sect. 7 concludes the paper.

2   Preliminaries

In the article, we use $u \leftarrow U$ to represent that an element u is selected from set U, and $u \xleftarrow{R} U$ to represent that an element u is selected from set U uniformly and randomly [14,23]. We use $\|$ to indicate string concatenation [14]. The main notations used in this article are listed in Table 1.

Table 1. Summary of notations

Notations	Denotations
G	A graph data set
I	A secure index
V	A set of all vertices of the graph G
$|V|$	The number of vertices of the graph G
$T(v_i)$	A set of all adjacency vertices of vertex $v_i(1 \leq i \leq |V|)$, the value of which is indicated as $|T(v_i)|$
max	The maximum degree of the graph G, that is, the maximum number of adjacency vertices
Q_{v_i}	A set of encrypted query tokens of vertex $v_i(1 \leq i \leq |V|)$, to prevent revealing the actual number of queries. The set contains max components, i.e., $Q_{v_i} = (q_{i1}, \ldots, q_{imax})$
R_{v_i}	A set of search results of vertex $v_i(1 \leq i \leq |V|)$,
$Enc_{key}(\cdot)$	A semantic security symmetric encryption function used in our scheme designing
$Dec_{key}(\cdot)$	A semantic security symmetric decryption function used in our scheme designing

To achieve the homoionym search, we use porter stem extraction algorithm which is usually adopted in information retrieval [24]. Of course, we can also use other algorithms to achieve this function in our scheme, not limited to this one. The set of vertices in a graph is represented as $V = \{v_1, \ldots, v_n\}$, and the set converted through stem extraction algorithm is $W = \{w_1, \ldots, w_m\}$. The number of elements in the set W is not greater than the number of elements in the set V, and the converted set of graph vertices can be used for querying.

3 Scheme Construction

3.1 Design Overview

In cloud computing, the query architecture model illustrated in Fig. 1 mainly consists of three parts: the cloud server, the data owner, and the user. The cloud server has storage and data processing capabilities, and the graph dataset and the constructed secure index are stored on the cloud server. The cloud server implements secure queries for users using security index. In the implementation of the scheme, we adopt the idea of searchable encryption, and assume that the

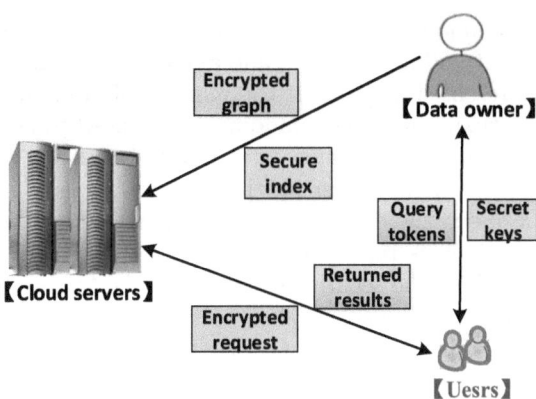

Fig. 1. Query architecture model over medical graph data in cloud computing

user has the authorization key to obtain the query request [14]. We agree to adopt an adaptive attack model for cloud servers in this article [14,16].

In the scheme of this article, The main task is to construct the index and encrypted query tokens, as well as how to implement queries. The algorithms involved in this scheme include secret key generation, index construction and query implementation.

3.2 Scheme Designing

We now build the AQHS scheme. Similar to the existing searchable encryption solutions [14,16], our querying mechanism can achieve the adjacency query supporting homoionym search over encrypted graph data.

The set of graph vertices is represented as $V = \{v_1, \ldots, v_n\}$. To implement the homoionym search, we use porter stem extraction algorithm to convert the graph vertex set to set $W = \{w_1, \ldots, w_m\}$. For each element $w_i \in W (1 \leq i \leq |W|)$, we build an array T_i containing the adjacency vertices, and $|T_i|$ represents the number of elements of the array T_i. To prevent the leakage of private information, the data owner encrypts the contents of the array elements. The adjacency array of all vertices in the graph is generated and represented by the set T.

After constructing the adjacency array, we need to build a secure index to implement adjacency queries. For an element $w_i (1 \leq i \leq |W|)$ in set W, the adjacency vertices related to it is stored in set T_i, and the number of the adjacency vertices is $|T_i|$. For $1 \leq j \leq |T_i|$, we create a tag for w_i by concatenating w_i with j, and the tag is denoted as $w_i || j$. After the creation is completed, the collection of all tags related to this element w_i is represented as $C_{w_i} = (w_i || 1, \ldots, w_i || |T_i|)$. The adjacency information corresponding to each element in set C_{w_i} is stored in the index. Searching for adjacent information related to w_i is equivalent to searching the index for elements related to all tags in set C_{w_i}. In this way, the information related to the vertices of the graph is associated with the query index. To hide the number of different adjacent vertices of each vertex in the graph, it is necessary to fill in the index, and assuming that the maximum degree of the graph is represented as max. If the number of adjacency vertices about the element w_i less than max, some padding values need to be added.

After we have built the adjacency array and the secure index, the secure index is stored on the cloud server so that it can be used to execute query. When executing a query, the data owner constructs the query token set for the query element w_i, which is represented as $Q_{w_i} = (q_{i1}, \ldots, q_{imax})$. The query token set is encrypted for the security reasons, that is, $Q_{w_i} = (q_{i1}, \ldots, q_{imax}) = (Enc_{s_i}(w_i \| 1), \ldots, Enc_{s_i}(v_i \| max))$. When a user wants to query the adjacency information of w_i, the query token set Q_{w_i} is sent to the cloud server. The cloud server uses this query token set to query the relevant items in the index and returns the query results to the user.

In this article, we use l and r to represent the security parameters used in the scheme construction. Our constructing process of the scheme about the adjacency query supporting homoionym search is described in Fig. 2.

KeyConstructing(l):

Generate random keys k_i, $s_i \xleftarrow{R} (0,1)^l$, where, $1 \leq i \leq max$.

ConstructingArray(G, k_i):

1. The set of all the vertexs in the graph G is $V = (v_1, \ldots, v_n)$.
2. The converted set of the set V is $W = (w_1, \ldots, w_m)$ by porter stem extraction algorithm.
3. Constructing an array C_i for the vertex $w_i \in W$, where, $1 \leq i \leq |W|$, and each entry in the array represents an edge.
4. For the array C_i ($1 \leq i \leq |W|$):
   (1) For $1 \leq j \leq |C_i|$:
       Set $w_{ij} = <Enc_{s_i}(value)>$, and set $C_i[j] = w_{ij}$. //Value is vertex information.
   (2) The element is encrypted, and get the encrypted array C_i.

ConstructingIndex(G, s_i):

1. For each element $C_i[j]$ in the array C_i, where, $1 \leq i \leq |W|$, $1 \leq j \leq |C_i|$,
   (1) Compute $position = Enc_{s_i}(w_i \| j)$;
   (2) Set $\mathbf{I}[position] = C_i[j]$.
2. For the array C_i, if $|C_i| < max$, then set ($max - |C_i|$) values in $\mathbf{I}$, and there exists exactly max adjacency vertex in $\mathbf{I}$ for each $w_i \in W$. This can be done as follows:
   (1) Let $x = |C_i|$ be the number of elements in $\mathbf{I}$ that already contain w_i;
   (2) For $1 \leq t \leq max-x$, compute $position = Enc_{s_i}(0^t \| (max + t))$, set $\mathbf{I}[position] = Enc_{s_i}(0 \| (|V| + t) \| 0^r)$.

ConstructingToken(w_i, s_i):

$Q_{w_i} = (q_{i1}, \ldots, q_{im}) = (Enc_{s_i}(w_i \| 1), \ldots, Enc_{s_i}(w_i \| max))$.

ExecutingQuery($\mathbf{I}$, Q_{w_i}):

1. For $1 \leq j \leq max$, if $\mathbf{I}(q_{ij})$ exists, then $\mathbf{I}(q_{ij})$ is added to the result set R_{w_i}.
2. Output the result set R_{w_i}.

Fig. 2. Scheme constructing process

4 Security Analysis

The security analysis of our scheme is given in this section. Our scheme follows the ideas and concepts of searchable symmetric encryption in the literature [12, 14, 16]. We use the simulation-based method in the security analysis [12,14]. We assume that the cloud server adopts an adaptive attack model, and an attacker cannot distinguish the views of the two histories [14]. The security theorem of our scheme about the adjacency query supporting homoionym search is stated below.

Theorem 1. Our AQHS scheme meets the adaptive semantic security.

Proof. To prove the semantic security of our scheme, we define a probabilistic polynomial-scale simulator S, and such that for all $q \in N$, S can simulate the attacker A. For all $0 \le t \le q$, given $T_r(H_q^t)$ of a partial history, the attacker S can generate a view $(V_q^t)^*$ such that $(V_q^t)^*$ is indistinguishable from $V_K^t(H_q)$ of A.

For $t = 0$, on the partial history $T_r(H_q^0)$, the simulator S constructs the simulated index $\mathbf{I}^*$ that contains $(|W| * max)$ entries to simulate the index $\mathbf{I}$, both of which are equally large in scale. For each element of the set W in the graph, $\mathbf{I}^*$ contains max copies of adjacency information inserted at random positions. The simulator S keeps a copy of $\mathbf{I}^*$ to be able to simulate future partial views for $0 \le t \le q$. It is obvious that $\mathbf{I}^*$ is indistinguishable from $\mathbf{I}$, otherwise the outputs of the symmetric encryption mechanism of semantic security can be distinguished from random strings of the same size. Thus, $(V_q^0)^*$ is indistinguishable from $V_K^0(H_q)$.

For $1 \le t \le q$, the simulator S can adopt the previously constructing index $\mathbf{I}^*$, and $T_r(H_q^t)$ contains the search pattern matrix for t queries. We next explain how the simulator S constructs the query tokens $(Q_1^*, \ldots, Q_t^*)$ included in $(V_q^t)^*$. In the process of constructing these tokens, the simulator S can reuse the tokens $(Q_1^*, \ldots, Q_{t-1}^*)$ that were included in $(V_q^{t-1})^*$. Alternatively, the simulator S can reconstruct these query tokens from $T_r(H_q^{t-1})$. We next explain how to construct Q_t^*.

To construct Q_t^*, the simulator S first checks whether H_q^{t-1} contains v_t by checking if its search pattern equals to 1 for any $1 \le j \le t - 1$. If it is not equal to 1, the simulator S makes use of the knowledge from $T_r(H_q^t)$ about R_{w_t}, that is $C_{v_t} = (C(w_t||1), \ldots, C(w_t||max))$. The simulator S constructs new encrypted information by selecting any string randomly. The simulator S randomly picks an address add_i from $\mathbf{I}^*$ for $1 \le i \le max$, insuring that all add_i are pairwise different, and constructs the query information $Q_t^* = (add_1, \ldots, add_{max})$. Otherwise, if H_q^{t-1} contains w_t, then the simulator S retrieves the query information associated with w_t and assigns it to Q_t^*. It ensures that if H_q^t contains query tokens, then the query tokens included in $(V_q^t)^*$ are also identical.

It is obvious that, the query tokens $(Q_1^*, \ldots, Q_t^*)$ in $(V_q^t)^*$ is indistinguishable from the query tokens $(Q_1, \ldots, Q_t)$ in $V_K^t(H_q)$, otherwise, the output of the symmetric encryption mechanism can be distinguished from a random string of the same size. So, for $0 \le t \le q$, $(V_q^t)^*$ and $V_K^t(H_q)$ are indistinguishable for polynomial-scale attacker. Therefore, the AQHS theorem has been proven to be of security.

5   Experimental Evaluations

This section analyzes our scheme through experimental comparison on the Enron email network graph [25, 26]. The experiment is implemented by the C program and executed on the server side and local platform. The local workstation runs Win10 and has an Intel Core 6 CPU running at 3.2 GHz, and 4 GB of RAM. The cloud server runs Linux and is equipped with 8 CPU cores and 16GB of RAM.

The performance evaluation of query execution based on secure index and query tokens is implemented on the cloud server side. Our scheme considers two scenarios for comparative analysis of its performance. One is to use the maximum degree under the best circumstance (shorter form MDB), that is $max = 2 \cdot |W| - 2$, where $|W|$ is the number of the converted set of graph vertices. The other is used in our AQHS, that is to say, max is the maximum value in the set of adjacency vertices.

During the execution of the query operation, the cloud server completes the retrieval through the index and the query tokens. The experimental evaluation is mainly to analyze and compare the query overhead to test the effectiveness of our scheme. The experimental results are plotted in Fig. 3, where the Y-axis of Fig. 3 represents the query time, and the X-axis represents the number of vertices or edges in the graph.

From the experimental results of Fig. 3, it can be observed that the query time is almost linear to the number of vertices or edges in the graph. In the query experiment, our scheme has the higher query efficiency, while also protecting the security of the query. Although our scheme goes through the steps of encryption operation and executes the query on the remote server side, it is acceptable from the overall effect.

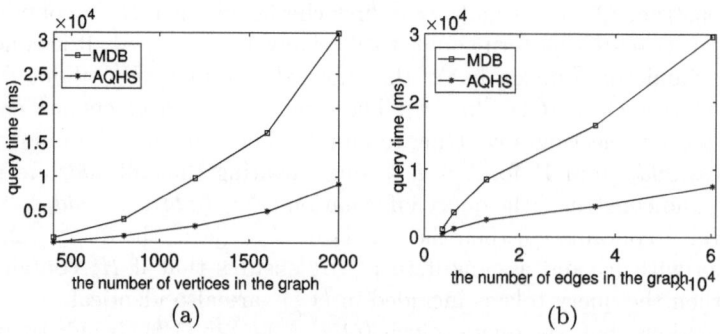

Fig. 3. Query execution time

In general, as can be seen from the results of the experimental analysis, the cost of our AQHS scheme is relatively small. At the same time, it also meets the requirements of security. The index construction of our scheme is built locally at one time. Considering the effective search over the encrypted graph data on the cloud server, it would be acceptable.

6   Related Work

For the query operation of outsourced data, there are two kinds of encryption search models: the asymmetrical search encryption model and the symmetric search encryption model [14, 15]. The execution efficiency of asymmetrical encryption model is far less efficient than that of the symmetrical encryption model [14–16]. Considering the higher efficiency of symmetric encryption, we use the idea of searchable symmetric encryption in this article.

The idea of searchable symmetric encryption was first proposed by Dawn Song, et al. in the literature [11], and it takes advantage of the stream cipher to encrypt all the words in each file. Goh [13] first introduced the notion of the secure index, which made use of a bloom filter to build an index for each file. There will be a false positive for searching in this scheme, and the searching cost is proportional to the number of files in the collection. Curtmola et al. [14] has built non-adaptive symmetric search encryption and adaptive asymmetrical search encryption schemes respectively. Boneh et al. studied the searchable encryption mechanism based on a public key cryptography algorithm and proposed the concept of public key encryption with keyword search for the first time [15]. With the continuous progress of research, some extended searchable encryption schemes have emerged [16–18]. These schemes have made some improvements in expanding the scope of queries and enhancing query functionality. But all the scheme are not directly used for the adjacency query supporting homoionym search vover the encrypted graph data.

In recent years, the query problem on outsourced graph data has attracted the attention of researchers, and some achievements have been made [19–22]. Chase et al. proposed the idea of structure encryption, and studied the query problem about graph structure data [19]. Cao et al. firstly studied and solved the problem of subgraph queries over outsourced graph data [20]. Shen et al. proposed a graph encryption scheme to implement constrained shortest distance queries and proposed a tree based ciphertext comparison protocol [21]. Ciucanu et al. designed and implemented a secure framework for outsourcing graph data to execute queries with SPARQL evaluation [22]. At present, for the query problem of our proposed adjacency query supporting homoionym search, existing methods cannot directly solve it. We need to design suitable solutions to handle and solve this problem.

7   Conclusion

This article provides a solution for secure query processing of outsourced medical graph data, which is an attempt to apply medical image data in cloud computing.

In this article, we give and handle the problem of adjacency query supporting homoionym search over medical graph data in cloud computing. For achieving the adjacency query, we use the idea of searchable symmetric encryption and the stem extraction algorithm to construct our query scheme. We achieve the homoionym search in the adjacency query, which greatly improves the scope and function of the query for the user. We prove the security of our scheme through formal analysis. The results of experimental analysis further demonstrate the efficiency of our scheme.

We will conduct research in this direction based on the current research. We will first consider combining with artificial intelligence algorithms to improve our execution efficiency. Then we will continue to study the implementation of query scheme while considering the dynamic changes in data.

Acknowledgment. The authors gratefully acknowledge the editor and the reviewers' comments and helpful suggestions. This research is supported in part by the National Nature Science Foundation of China (No. 62262033 and 62062045).

References

1. Sampe, J., Artigas, M.S., Vernik, G., et al.: Outsourcing data processing jobs with Lithops. IEEE Trans. Cloud Comput. **11**(1), 1026–1037 (2023)
2. Li, J., Ye, H., et al.: Efficient and secure outsourcing of differentially private data publishing with multiple evaluators. IEEE Trans. Dependable Sec. Comput. **19**(1), 109–121 (2022)
3. Ren, Y., Song, Z., Sun, S., et al.: Outsourcing lda-based face recognition to an untrusted cloud. IEEE Trans. Dependable Sec. Comput. **23**(3), 2058–2070 (2023)
4. Liu, W., Wen, D., Wang, H., et al.: Skyline nearest neighbor search on multi-layer graphs. In: 2014 IEEE 35th International Conference on Data Engineering Workshops, pp. 259-265. IEEE, Piscataway, N.J., USA (2019)
5. Potamias, M., Bonchi, F., Gionis, A., et al.: K-nearest neighbors in uncertain graphs. Proc/ VLDB Endowment **3**(1), 997–1008 (2010)
6. Wang, R., Yan, J., Yang, X., et al.: Combinatorial learning of robust deep graph matching: an embedding based approach. IEEE Trans. Pattern Anal. Mach. Intell. **45**(6), 6984–7000 (2023)
7. Bazgan, C., Pontoizeau, T., Tuza, Z., et al.: Finding a potential community in networks. Theoret. Comput. Sci. **769**, 32–42 (2019)
8. Ferrer-Cid, P., Barceló-Ordinas, J., García-Vidal, J., et al.: Volterra graph-based outlier detection for air pollution sensor networks. IEEE Trans. Netw. Sci. Eng. **9**(4), 2759–2771 (2023)
9. Li, X., Ye, H., Li, T., et al.: Efficient and secure outsourcing of differentially private data publishing with multiple evaluators. IEEE Trans. Dependable Secure Comput. **19**(1), 67–76 (2022)
10. Zhang, X., Zhao, J., Xu, C., et al.: DOPIV: post-quantum secure identity-based data outsourcing with public integrity verification in cloud storage. IEEE Trans. Serv. Comput. **15**(1), 334–345 (2022)
11. Song, D.X., Wagner, D., Perrig, A.: Practical techniques for searches on encrypted data. In: Proceeding: IEEE Symposium on Security and Privacy (S&P 2000), vol. 2000, pp. 44–55. IEEE: Los Alamitos, CA, USA (2000)

12. Chang, Y.-C., Mitzenmacher, M.: Privacy preserving keyword searches on remote encrypted data. In: Ioannidis, J., Keromytis, A., Yung, M. (eds.) ACNS 2005. LNCS, vol. 3531, pp. 442–455. Springer, Heidelberg (2005). https://doi.org/10.1007/11496137_30

13. Goh, E.J.: Secure indexes. In: Cryptology ePrint Archive, Report 2003/216 (2003)

14. Curtmola, R., Garay, J., Kamara, S., et al.: Searchable symmetric encryption: improved definitions and efficient constructions. In: Proceedings of the 13th ACM Conference on Computer and Communications Security (CCS 2006), pp. 79-88. ACM, Alexandria, VA, United States (2006)

15. Baek, J., Safavi-Naini, R., Susilo, W.: Public key encryption with keyword search revisited. In: Gervasi, O., Murgante, B., Laganà, A., Taniar, D., Mun, Y., Gavrilova, M.L. (eds.) ICCSA 2008. LNCS, vol. 5072, pp. 1249–1259. Springer, Heidelberg (2008). https://doi.org/10.1007/978-3-540-69839-5_96

16. Cao, N., Wang, C., Li, M., et al.: Privacy-preserving multi-keyword ranked search over encrypted cloud data. In: IEEE Conference on Computer Communications (INFOCOM 2011), pp. 829-837. IEEE: Shanghai, China (2011)

17. Mei, Z., Yu, J., Zhang, C., et al.: Secure multi-dimensional data retrieval with access control and range query in the cloud. Inf. Syst. **122**, 102343 (2024)

18. Wang, C., Ren, K., Yu, S., et al. Achieving usable and privacy-assured similarity search over outsourced cloud data. In: IEEE Conference on Computer Communications (INFOCOM 2012), pp. 451-459. IEEE: Orlando, FL, USA (2012)

19. Chase, M., Kamara, S., et al.: Structured encryption and controlled disclosure. structured encryption and controlled disclosure. Cryptol. Inform. Sec. **2010**, 577-594 (2010)

20. Cao, N., Yang, Z., Wang, C., et al.: Privacy-preserving query over encrypted graph-structured data in cloud computing. In: Proceedings of the 2011 31st International Conference on Distributed Computing Systems (ICDCS 2011), pp. 393 - 402. IEEE, Los Alamitos, CA, USA (2011)

21. Shen, M., Ma, B., Zhu, L., et al.: Cloud-based approximate constrained shortest distance queries over encrypted graphs with privacy protection. IEEE Trans. Inf. Forensics Secur. **13**, 940–953 (2018)

22. Ciucanu, R., Lafourcade, P.: GOOSE: a secure framework for graph outsourcing and SPARQL evaluation. In: Singhal, A., Vaidya, J. (eds.) DBSec 2020. LNCS, vol. 12122, pp. 347–366. Springer, Cham (2020). https://doi.org/10.1007/978-3-030-49669-2_20

23. Katz, J., Lindell, Y.: Introduction to Modern Cryptography. Chapman & Hall/CRC (2007)

24. Singhal, A.: Modern information retrieval: a brief overview. Bull. IEEE Comput. Soc. Tech. Committee Data Eng. **24**(4), 35–43 (2001)

25. Leskovec, J., Lang, K.J., Dasgupta, A., et al.: Community structure in large networks: natural cluster sizes and the absence of large well-defined clusters. Internet Math. **6**(1), 29–123 (2009)

26. Klimt, B., Yang, Y.: Introducing the Enron corpus. In: First Conference on Email and Anti-Spam (CEAS 2004), pp. 1-2. Google, Microsoft, etc.: Mountain View, CA, USA (2004)

ADAPT: Attention-Driven Domain Adaptation for Inter-cluster Workload Forecasting in Cloud Data Centers

Nosin Ibna Mahbub[1], Afsana Kabir Sinthia[1], Mincheol Jeon[1], Junyoung Park[2], and Eui-Nam Huh[1(✉)]

[1] Department of Computer Science and Engineering,Kyung Hee University, Yongin-si, Gyeonggi-do, Republic of Korea
{nimahbub,afsana,2019102224,johnhuh}@khu.ac.kr
[2] Korea Institute of Science and Technology Information, Daejeon, Republic of Korea
jypark@kisti.re.kr

Abstract. Cloud computing has recently gained popularity due to its cost-effective and high-quality services. Cloud-native systems are expected to host more than 95% of digital workloads. Cloud service providers face two significant challenges: real-time workload predictions and effective resource management. Furthermore, allocating resources over time may result in a suboptimal execution environment due to considerable increases and decreases in workload that follow time-dependent patterns. Recent breakthroughs in deep learning have garnered widespread favor for predicting extremely nonlinear cloud workloads; nevertheless, they have been unable to generalize inter cluster workload forecasting due to inadequate workload data at the beginning of each cluster. Furthermore, the distribution disparity across distinct cluster workloads is caused by a variety of elements, making it difficult to reuse current data or models directly. To overcome these challenges, we propose **ADAPT**, which relies on **A**ttention-Driven **D**omain **Adapt**ation. First, we use LSTM architecture as the backbone of our model. Moreover, we construct a strategically shared attention module to transmit relevant knowledge from the source domain to the target domain by inducing domain-invariant latent features and retraining domain-specific features. Lastly, adversarial training is used to increase the model's resilience and predictive accuracy. Comprehensive experimental evaluations indicate that our proposed approach significantly outperforms existing baselines.

Keywords: Cloud computing · Workload prediction · Domain adaption

1 Introduction

Cloud computing is an essential component of current IT infrastructure, and it is growing at a rapid pace. According to data, the worldwide cloud comput-

Y. Wang and L.-J. Zhang (Eds.): CLOUD 2024, LNCS 15423, pp. 56–68, 2025.
https://doi.org/10.1007/978-3-031-77153-8_6

ing industry would be worth $602.31 billion by 2023. Until 2030, the market is estimated to increase at a Compound Annual Growth Rate (CAGR) of 21.2% [28]. That demand has skyrocketed during the COVID-19 epidemic, when working from home has become increasingly popular. Advances in Artificial Intelligence (AI) and Big Data have driven more enterprises to use cloud computing solutions, resulting in an increasing demand for these technologies. Workload forecasting and scheduling are critical in determining the cost of running data centers, yet estimating resource demand is difficult [21]. Furthermore, data centers have a big effect on the environment. Accordingly, the power usage of data centers will rise from 292 TWh in 2016 to 353 TWh in 2030 as a result of an increase in users. If this growth in energy consumption is not reined in, ICT-related greenhouse gas emissions could rise to over 14% in 2040 as opposed to a range of 1.6% to 1.6% between 2007 and 2016 [28]. Cloud computing companies try to provide a good Quality of Service (QoS) by preconfiguring the machines. Usually, cloud environments are made up of different devices. As a result, the total computing burden was dynamic and diverse by nature [14]. Problems including trouble allocating resources, breaking Service-Level Agreements (SLAs), wasting resources, and inefficient use of money are caused by these traits. These problems jeopardize cloud infrastructures' effective functioning and QoS. Specifically, inefficient use of resources and SLA breaches can result from under- or over-provisioning, which is a prevalent practice in cloud resource allocation [16]. Predicting future demand also has the advantage of improving resource usage and reducing over allocation while offering the chance to serve a larger client base. This increases profit and lowers total energy consumption, CO2 emissions, and maintenance costs. With an emphasis on probabilistic and uncertain elements, machine learning (ML) and deep learning (DL) techniques have been widely employed to estimate future demand in the cloud environment [11,17,24]. Usually, cloud providers oversee several clusters, each with distinct properties, resource requirements, and workload patterns. Even within the same cloud provider, resource utilization trends might vary greatly between clusters and datacenters. Traditional machine learning or deep learning models are challenged by these variances as they frequently presume that the data used for training and testing come from a similar distribution. Domain adaptation (DA) strategies have shown great promise in mitigating the detrimental effects of domain shift by aligning features from the source and target domains [8,13]. While similar strategies have been successfully used to image data, there has been less study on adaption methods for time series data, which is frequently more complicated due to its predictive character than classification [23]. In present methods, classifiers use source domain data to learn domain-invariant features and map labels in the latent space [9]. This strategy allows the classifier to take common information from multiple domains and apply it to the target domain. However, applying these techniques to cloud workload forecasting data remains difficult. In contrast, workload prediction tasks require flexible output spaces, which are frequently domain-specific. As a result, there is a need for enhanced models that can effectively capture both long-term and short-term dependencies, as well as the development of new domain adaptation approaches tailored to time series prediction.

To address the aforementioned issues, we propose a cloud workload forecasting model that utilizes domain adaptation and attention sharing. Initially, we present a domain adaption technique for learning domain-invariant data from related datasets, followed by the construction of a shared attention module with the LSTM network. This section captures domain-invariant and domain-specific characteristics, which are subsequently combined into predictions to simulate domain-related traits and accurately estimate the relevant domains' data distributions. Furthermore, we use adversarial training in the model in order to more accurately represent the long-term reliance of workload. We improve the global prediction accuracy and data representation by incorporating a discriminator into the data distribution model. The primary contributions of this study are outlined as follows:

- We propose ADAPT, a novel framework that utilizes domain adaptation and attention mechanisms to tackle the challenges of inter-cluster resource allocation in cloud data centers.
- We construct a systematically shared attention module to facilitate successful knowledge transfer between source and destination domains, allowing the model to accumulate domain-invariant features while retraining domain-specific ones.
- Adversarial training is adopted to enhance the model's robustness to fluctuations in workload distributions, resulting in higher predicted accuracy in diverse cloud environments.
- We conduct comprehensive experiments to evaluate the efficacy of our proposed method, and the results show that our proposed approach considerably surpasses existing baseline methods in terms of cloud workload prediction.

The remaining sections of the paper are organized as follows. In Sect. 2, the literature review is covered in details. Section 3 provides a detailed design and implementation process for the proposed ADAPT. Section 4 presents ADAPT's experimental results on two real-world trace datasets, as well as comparisons with alternative baselines. Section 5 concludes this study.

2   Literature Review

2.1   Cloud Workload Forecasting

For the past two decades, cloud workload forecasting has been an increasingly important concern in cloud computing management. Existing methodologies can be roughly classified as statistical and machine learning (ML) methods, deep learning (DL) techniques, or hybrid systems. Traditional statistical and machine learning approaches including Holt-Winters [19], ARIMA [27], SARIMA [15], Markov models [4], and feed-forward neural networks [2] are commonly used.

While these techniques have shown potential, they frequently encounter non-linearities in time-series data and overlook long-term relationships in resource utilization indicators [2].

The advent of deep learning has prompted the investigation of several architectures for workload prediction. Convolutional Neural Networks (CNNs) and Long Short-Term Memory (LSTM) networks outperformed older approaches, both separately and in combination [12]. Attention mechanisms and encoder-decoder models have improved prediction accuracy, especially for CPU workload forecasting [25]. Recent developments indicate a preference for ensemble models, which mix different architectures to capture diverse features of workload traces. For example, hybrid models that combine Random Forests with LSTM [22] and Generative Adversarial Networks with LSTM [26] have demonstrated promising results in both one-step-ahead and multi-step-ahead predictions.

Despite these advances, most existing research assumes sufficient historical trace data for training and uniform distribution among clusters, which may not be applicable to cloud computing systems in the actual world. This identifies a huge research gap regarding the development of inter-cluster workload forecasting methods.

2.2 Deep Domain Adaptation Methods

Furthermore, the area of unsupervised domain adaptation has made substantial progress in dealing with domain changes in distribution and feature spaces. Early methods concentrated on reweighting source example losses [10], but subsequent approaches investigated subspace alignment and moment matching with techniques such as Maximum Mean Discrepancy [6] and Correlation Alignment [20]. In the context of regression problems, domain adaptation research has established point-wise loss guarantees for kernel-based regularization methods and investigated factorizing multivariate density into bivariate copula functions. Recent work has developed domain-invariant Partial-Least-Squares Regression using domain regularizes. However, domain adaptation for regression using temporal multivariate data is a relatively unexplored topic [1], giving prospects for future study in cloud workload forecasting.

3 Proposed Methodology

3.1 Problem Formulation

Consider a collection of recorded cloud workload $W = [w_1, w_2...w_T] \in \mathbb{R}^{(NT)}$ where T is the overall length of this workload, N is the feature dimension and $W_j = [w_j^1, w_j^2...w_j^N]^T \in \mathbb{R}^{(N)}$ is utilized to identify a 1D tensor of N workload at time j. The predictive workload $W^p = \{x_j^1, j = 1, 2, ..., T\}$ is the most representative of the N attribute workloads, whereas the remaining workloads $W^{NP} = \{[w_j^2, w_j^3, ..., w_j^N]^T, j = 1, 2, ..., T\}$ are non-predictive. The sliding window approach is frequently utilized when producing dataset $D = \{(\mathbb{W}_i, y_i)\}_{i=1}^N$

for multivariate cloud workload prediction problems where N is the size of the dataset. In particular, $\mathbb{W} = [w_i, w_{i+1}, ...w_{i+z-1}] \in \mathbb{R}^{NXZ}$, where Z is the number of time frames and indicates the value of the forecasted time series in the future k^{th} step, where $k \geq 1$.

The purpose is to transfer knowledge from a multivariate cloud workload with a source domain to a target domain for more accurate forecasting outcomes. This work focuses on homogeneous transfer learning, which involves the source domain $D_s = (\mathbb{W}_i^s, y_i^s)_{i=1}^{N_s}$ and target domain $D_t = (\mathbb{W}_j^t, y_j^t)_{j=1}^{N_t}$.

3.2   Architecture of ADAPT

This section describes the architecture of the time series forecasting approach, which uses attention-led domain adaptation (ADAPT). Figure 1 illustrates overall architecture of our proposed approach. The primary component of our suggested method is the LSTM [18] model. The domain discriminator and the shared attention module are the two major components of ADAPT. For adaptation, both domains share a common attention module. Additionally, global adversarial training via the domain discriminator improves predicting performance.

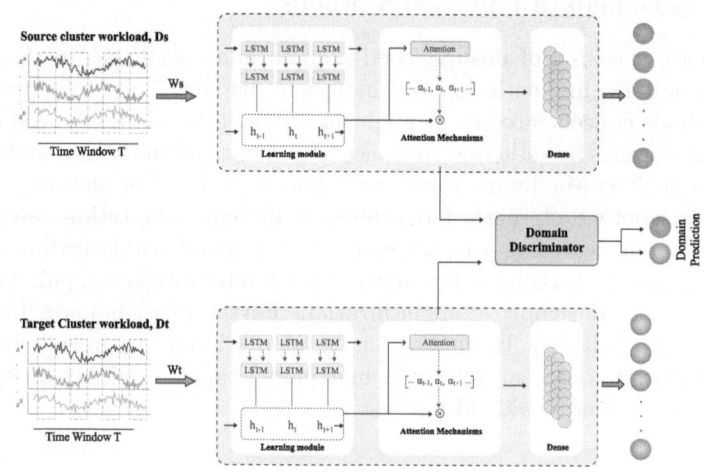

Fig. 1. An Architectural Overview of the Proposed ADAPT Method

Attention Sharing. For cloud workload prediction tasks, the shared attention unit aims to transfer knowledge from a source domain to a target domain. Considering the features of time series forecasting jobs, this method exchanges domain-invariant features via a shared attention module and keeps the LSTM blocks privately stored by the relevant domain. The specifics of the implementation are as follows: The time series data is fed into an LSTM block first, followed by an attention block, which generates queries $\mathbf{Q}$ and keys $\mathbf{K}$. The shared attention module is then given the resulting domain-invariant queries $\mathbf{Q}$ and keys $\mathbf{K}$. To be more specific, we use a position-wise MLP to project $\mathbf{Q}$ and $\mathbf{K}$ into a d-dimensional vector where θ represents the parameters.

$$(q_t, k_t) = MLP(Q, K; \theta_s) \tag{1}$$

Consequently, after normalizing the positions, an attention score is computed using a positive semi-definite kernel function called $\mathcal{K}(\cdot, \cdot)$:

$$\alpha(q_t, k_{t'}) = \frac{\mathcal{K}(q_t, k_{t'})}{\sum_{t' \in \mathcal{N}(t)} \mathcal{K}(q_t, k_{t'})} \tag{2}$$

here, the kernel function calculates the similarity between q_t, and $k_{t'}$, and the attention score is normalized over the set of surrounding positions $\mathcal{N}(t)$.

Adversarial Training. This study examines the challenge of cloud workload forecasting by framing it as the task of identifying an appropriate forecasting model $\mathcal{M}$ on a data space time series dataset. We have sample target data D_t and source data D_s in this domain adaptation challenge. Our goal is to produce a workload prediction on the target domain $\mathcal{T}$ that is more accurate. Motivated by the Generative Adversarial Network (GAN) [5] concept, we employ adversarial training to enhance global forecasting performance. The goal of our approach is to increase the likelihood that the ground truth and forecast values will be correctly labeled. The neural network's loss is:

$$\min_{L_s, L_t} \max_D \mathcal{L}_b(D_s, L_s) + \mathcal{L}(D_t; L_t) - \lambda \mathcal{L}_d(D_s, D_t; D, L_s, L_t), \tag{3}$$

where D stands for a discriminator that seeks to identify the domain from which the sample originates, and L_s and L_t are LSTM blocks that estimate prediction values in each domain, respectively. In addition, $\mathcal{L}$ represents the agent prediction network's loss, which is comprised of the Kullback-Leibler (KL) [7] divergence and the fundamental cross-entropy loss to match the expected distribution:

$$\mathcal{L}_b(D; L) = \sum_{i=1}^{N} (\frac{1}{T} \sum_{t=T+1}^{T+t} l(y_i, t, y'_{i,t})) + D_{KL}(Y_{true}(y) \| Y'_{pred}(y)) \tag{4}$$

Error in domain classification in the latent spaces, $\mathcal{L}_d$ represents the cross-entropy loss as follows:

$$\mathcal{L}_d = -\frac{1}{N_d} \sum_{n=1}^{N_d} y_n log(y_n) + (1 - d_n) log(1 - z'_n) \tag{5}$$

Adversarial training is used to iteratively optimize the minimax objective, which is presented in Eq. 3. In Sect. 4, we go into further depth on the training process.

Algorithm 1 Adversarial Training for ADAPT

Require: Source domain data D_s, Target domain data D_t, LSTM blocks L_s and L_t,
    Domain discriminator D, Hyperparameter λ
Ensure: Trained model with improved global forecasting performance
1: **while** not converged **do**
2:     // Update Domain Discriminator
3:     $\mathcal{L}_d \leftarrow -\frac{1}{N_d}\sum_{n=1}^{N_d} y_n \log(y_n) + (1 - d_n)\log(1 - z_n')$
4:     Maximize $\mathcal{L}_d$ with respect to D
5:     // Update LSTM blocks
6:     $\mathcal{L}_b(D_s; L_s) \leftarrow \sum_{i=1}^{N}(\frac{1}{T}\sum_{t=T+1}^{T+t} l(y_i, t, y_{i,t}')) + D_{KL}(Y_{true}(y)||Y_{pred}'(y))$
7:     $\mathcal{L}_b(D_t; L_t) \leftarrow \sum_{i=1}^{N}(\frac{1}{T}\sum_{t=T+1}^{T+t} l(y_i, t, y_{i,t}')) + D_{KL}(Y_{true}(y)||Y_{pred}'(y))$
8:     // Minimax Optimization
9:     Minimize $\mathcal{L}_b(D_s; L_s) + \mathcal{L}_b(D_t; L_t) - \lambda\mathcal{L}_d$ with respect to L_s and L_t
10: **end while**
11: **return** Trained L_s, L_t, and D

The overall adversarial training procedure used by ADAPT for cloud workload prediction is described in Algorithm 1. Considering both source and target domains, iterative updates are made to an LSTM block and a domain discriminator. While LSTM blocks decrease a combined loss function, the discriminator increases the loss associated with domain categorization. This function incorporates an adversarial term and prediction mistakes, enabling the model to learn domain-invariant features. Through the process of enabling knowledge transfer from source to target domain, the technique enhances cloud workload forecast accuracy.

4   Experiments

This section compares our proposed ADAPT technique for predicting cloud workloads to baseline approaches using real-world datasets.

4.1   Experimental Datasets

We conduct the evaluation using four datasets from two real-world trace datasets. In all, four datasets were employed in our experiments: two clusters from Google Cloud trace 2019, one from Alibaba Cloud trace 2018, and one from Alibaba Cloud trace 2020.

Google Trace 2019: Google provided a dataset that tracks resource use across eight global cluster cells over 29 d, with around 10,000 computers per cell. It consists of a time series of average CPU and memory utilization at 5-minute intervals, including 8,352 data points. Missing records are disregarded, and the data is scaled between 0 and 1 using MinMax scaling to accelerate training convergence. The first cluster dataset is utilized as the source domain, while the second is used as the target domain.

Table 1. Results of CPU usage forecasting on the Alibaba trace dataset with sequence lengths $\in \{12, 24\}$. A lower MSE implies better performance, with the best outcomes displayed in bold.

Sequence Length	Methods	MSE	MAE	RMSE
12	LSTM-S	0.0193	0.1009	0.1389
	LSTM-FT	0.0168	0.0942	0.1295
	TF-S	0.8764	0.7092	0.9361
	TF-FT	0.7762	0.6125	0.8023
	R-DANN	0.0147	0.0951	0.1212
	ADAPT	**0.0131**	**0.0834**	**0.1142**
24	LSTM-S	0.0191	0.1010	0.1423
	LSTM-FT	0.0190	0.0952	0.1355
	TF-S	0.9486	0.7367	0.9739
	TF-FT	0.8126	0.7125	0.8122
	R-DANN	0.0239	0.0950	0.1122
	ADAPT	**0.0180**	**0.0724**	**0.1042**

Alibaba Trace 2018 and 2020: The 2018 trace records CPU and memory consumption over 8 d for around 4,000 computers, whereas the 2020 trace covers two months for 1,800 machines, including 6,500 GPUs. Data preparation takes the same approach as Google Cloud Trace. The source domain in this case is the 2020 dataset, while the target domain is the 2018 dataset.

4.2 Experimental Settings

All the experiments were carried out using a single GeForce RTX 3080 32GB GPU. We predict demand 10 min ahead at 5-minute intervals, which is appropriate for applications such as resource allocation and vertical scaling. Models were assessed with sequence lengths 12, 24. For each dataset, 80% was utilized for training and 20% for validation. 100 epochs were used to train the models with an early stopping patience of 15, followed by 10 epochs of fine-tuning with an early stopping patience of 2. The Adam optimizer was utilized using a learning rate of 0.0001 along with a batch size of 64 to train all the models. Mean Squared Error (MSE) was employed as the loss function during training. However, the metrics mean square error (RMSE), mean absolute error (MAE), and mean square error (MSE) were used for testing.

$$RMSE = \sqrt{\frac{1}{N}\sum_{t=1}^{N}(w'_t - w_t)^2} \tag{6}$$

$$MAE = \frac{1}{N}\sum_{t=1}^{N}|w'_t - w_t| \tag{7}$$

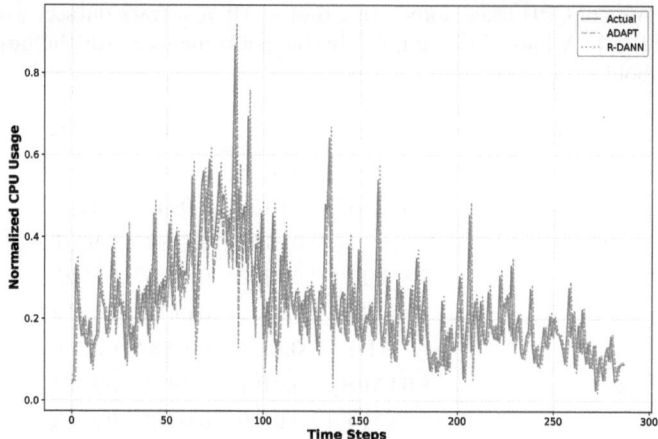

Fig. 2. The cpu usage prediction curve for Alibaba trace.

$$MSE = \frac{1}{N} \sum_{t=1}^{N} (w'_t - w_t)^2 \tag{8}$$

where w' is the predictive workload value, w denotes the actual workload, and N represents the total number of workload predicted samples.

4.3   Baseline Methods

- **LSTM-S.** A vanilla LSTM (Long Short-Term Memory) model trained on the source dataset and evaluated directly on the target dataset without any fine-tuning.
- **LSTM-FT:** An LSTM model that is trained on the source dataset, fine-tuned on the target dataset and evaluated on the target test set.
- **TF-S:** A Transformer model trained on the source dataset and tested on the target dataset without any fine-tuning.
- **TF-FT:** A Transformer model is trained on the source dataset, fine-tuned on the target dataset, and tested on the target test set
- **R-DANN:** R-DANN [3] is an unsupervised domain adaptation method that combines a Gradient Reversal Layer (GRL) and LSTM to provide a simple strategy for converting time series data from one domain to another.

4.4   Results and Analysis

Table 1 shows the experimental results for the Alibaba trace. As demonstrated in Table 1, ADAPT outperformed other baselines in both 12 and 24 sequence lengths. Based on the findings, it is confirmed that our proposed ADAPT has better adaption capabilities than other baselines. Figure 2 depicts the prediction results of CPU usages from an Alibaba trace with a sequence length of 12 using

Table 2. Results of CPU usage forecasting on the Google trace dataset with sequence lengths $\in \{12, 24\}$. A lower MSE implies better performance, with the best outcomes displayed in bold.

Sequence Length	Methods	MSE	MAE	RMSE
12	LSTM-S	0.0172	0.0942	0.1512
	LSTM-FT	0.0170	0.0823	0.1311
	TF-S	0.3109	0.1662	0.4077
	TF-FT	0.2722	0.1423	0.4011
	R-DANN	0.0118	0.0795	0.1132
	ADAPT	**0.0106**	**0.0721**	**0.1025**
24	LSTM-S	0.0156	0.0978	0.1963
	LSTM-FT	0.0153	0.0932	0.1736
	TF-S	0.1584	0.3077	0.3980
	TF-FT	0.1211	0.3100	0.3875
	R-DANN	0.0145	0.0752	0.1725
	ADAPT	**0.0130**	**0.0612**	**0.1423**

our proposed ADAPT approach and R-DANN (which performs second best). As shown in Fig. 2, the shifting trend of the ADAPT prediction curve is the most similar to the real curve. Quantitatively, ADAPT shows 32.12%, 22.02%, and 10.88% lower MSE than LSTM-S, LSTM-FT, and R-DANN respectively for sequence lengths of 12. We disregard transformer comparisons since they exhibit significantly lower performance than other models. Similarly, the experimental results on the Google Trace dataset, presented in Table 2, indicate that our proposed ADAPT model outperforms all the baselines in both 12 and 24 sequence lengths as well. To give a detailed comparison, Fig. 3 depicts the predicted CPU usage patterns using the ADAPT approach and the R-DNN model. As seen in Fig. 3, the prediction curve of ADAPT also closely resembles the actual CPU usage for Google trace. ADAPT reduced MSE by 38.37%, 37.65%, and 10.17% compared to the LSTM-S, LSTM-FT, and R-DANN models, respectively, proving its effectiveness in dealing with cross-cluster domain fluctuations in cloud data centers.

The results indicate that LSTM models outperform Transformer models, may be in conditions with short history lengths and little datasets. LSTMs successfully capture temporal dependencies inherent in cloud workload data, but Transformers, which rely on self-attention processes, fail to represent these dependencies in the absence of adequate data or fine-tuning. Furthermore, the R-DANN model outperforms both the LSTM and Transformer models by matching feature distributions across the source and target domains, resulting in better generalization to the target dataset. Furthermore, our proposed strategy is based on attention sharing and domain adaptation, which further enhances performance by efficiently collecting domain-specific information while using shared attention

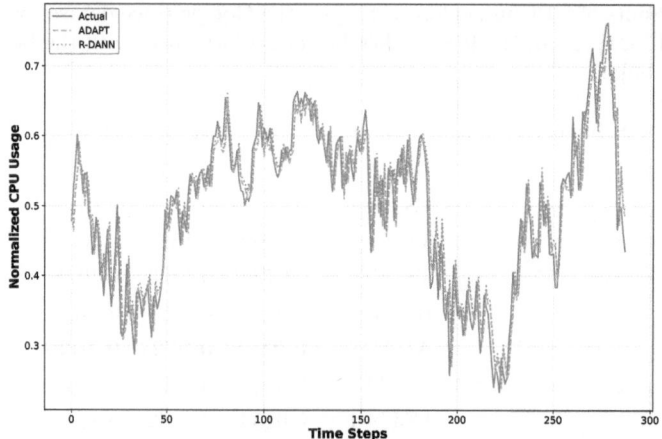

Fig. 3. The cpu usage prediction curve for Google trace

processes across domains. Our proposed strategy surpasses all baselines by combining the capabilities of attention mechanisms for detecting complicated patterns and domain adaptability for minimizing domain transitions. This enables more exact and robust modeling of cloud workload data, especially in transfer learning scenarios where domain-specific details are crucial for effective predictions.

5   Conclusion

This research introduced ADAPT, an effective approach for tackling the key topic of cross-cluster domain adaptation in cloud datacenter workload prediction. Adversarial training combined with attention-driven processes allows ADAPT to effectively transfer knowledge across the source and target domains. Experiments using Alibaba and Google trace datasets show that ADAPT outperforms traditional techniques, reducing MSE by up to 32.12% and 38.37% respectively. This large improvement in cross-cluster forecast accuracy allows for more efficient resource allocation and energy management across a variety of datacenter scenarios. ADAPT's ability to capture domain-invariant properties while adjusting to cluster-specific characteristics is a significant step forward in cloud computing operations. Future research will look into ADAPT's applicability to different workload types and real-time resource management scenarios, expanding its potential to improve flexibility and efficiency in complex cloud ecosystems.

Acknowledgments. This research was partly supported by the 1) Korea Institute of Science and Technology Information(KISTI) 2) Institute of Information & communications Technology Planning & Evaluation (IITP) grant funded by the Korea government(MSIT) (No. RS-2023-00220631, Edge Cloud Reference Architecture Standardization for Low Latency and Lightweight Cloud Service).

References

1. Aswolinskiy, W., Hammer, B.: Unsupervised transfer learning for time series via self-predictive modelling-first results. In: Proceedings of the Workshop on New Challenges in Neural Computation (NC2), vol. 3 (2017)
2. Caglar, F., Gokhale, A.: ioverbook: intelligent resource-overbooking to support soft real-time applications in the cloud. In: 2014 IEEE 7th International Conference on Cloud Computing, pp. 538–545. IEEE (2014)
3. da Costa, P.R.d.O., Akçay, A., Zhang, Y., Kaymak, U.: Remaining useful lifetime prediction via deep domain adaptation. Reliability Eng. Syst. Safety **195**, 106682 (2020)
4. Gong, Z., Gu, X., Wilkes, J.: Press: predictive elastic resource scaling for cloud systems. In: 2010 International Conference on Network and Service Management, pp. 9–16. IEEE (2010)
5. Goodfellow, I., et al.: Generative adversarial networks. Commun. ACM **63**(11), 139–144 (2020)
6. Gretton, A., Borgwardt, K., Rasch, M., Schölkopf, B., Smola, A.: A kernel method for the two-sample-problem. Adv. Neural Inform. Process. Syst. **19** (2006)
7. Hershey, J.R., Olsen, P.A.: Approximating the kullback leibler divergence between gaussian mixture models. In: 2007 IEEE International Conference on Acoustics, Speech and Signal Processing-ICASSP 2007, vol. 4, pp. IV–317. IEEE (2007)
8. Hoffman, J., et al.: Cycada: cycle-consistent adversarial domain adaptation. In: International Conference on Machine Learning, pp. 1989–1998. PMLR (2018)
9. Hu, H., Tang, M., Bai, C.: Datsing: data augmented time series forecasting with adversarial domain adaptation. In: Proceedings of the 29th ACM International Conference on Information & Knowledge Management, pp. 2061–2064 (2020)
10. Jiang, J., Zhai, C.: Instance weighting for domain adaptation in nlp. ACL (2007)
11. Kim, Y.M., Song, S., Koo, B.M., Son, J., Lee, Y., Baek, J.G.: Enhancing long-term cloud workload forecasting framework: Anomaly handling and ensemble learning in multivariate time series. IEEE Trans. Cloud Comput. (2024)
12. Leka, H.L., Fengli, Z., Kenea, A.T., Tegene, A.T., Atandoh, P., Hundera, N.W.: A hybrid cnn-lstm model for virtual machine workload forecasting in cloud data center. In: 2021 18th International Computer Conference on Wavelet Active Media Technology and Information Processing (ICCWAMTIP), pp. 474–478. IEEE (2021)
13. Long, M., Cao, Z., Wang, J., Jordan, M.I.: Conditional adversarial domain adaptation. Adv. Neural Inform. Process. Syst. **31** (2018)
14. Patel, Y.S., Bedi, J.: Mag-d: a multivariate attention network based approach for cloud workload forecasting. Futur. Gener. Comput. Syst. **142**, 376–392 (2023)
15. Podolskiy, V., Jindal, A., Gerndt, M., Oleynik, Y.: Forecasting models for self-adaptive cloud applications: a comparative study. In: 2018 ieee 12th international conference on self-adaptive and self-organizing systems (SASO), pp. 40–49. IEEE (2018)
16. Roy, N., Dubey, A., Gokhale, A.: Efficient autoscaling in the cloud using predictive models for workload forecasting. In: 2011 IEEE 4th International Conference on Cloud Computing, pp. 500–507. IEEE (2011)
17. Saxena, D., Kumar, J., Singh, A.K., Schmid, S.: Performance analysis of machine learning centered workload prediction models for cloud. IEEE Trans. Parallel Distrib. Syst. **34**(4), 1313–1330 (2023)
18. Sherstinsky, A.: Fundamentals of recurrent neural network (RNN) and long short-term memory (LSTM) network. Physica D **404**, 132306 (2020)

19. Subramanian, S., Kannammal, A.: Real time non-linear cloud workload forecasting using the holt-winter model. In: 2019 10th International Conference on Computing, Communication and Networking Technologies (ICCCNT), pp. 1–6. IEEE (2019)

20. Sun, B., Feng, J., Saenko, K.: Return of frustratingly easy domain adaptation. In: Proceedings of the AAAI Conference On Artificial Intelligence, vol. 30 (2016)

21. Tirmazi, M., et al.: Borg: the next generation. In: Proceedings of the Fifteenth European Conference on Computer Systems, pp. 1–14 (2020). https://doi.org/10.1145/3342195.338751

22. Valarmathi, K., Kanaga Suba Raja, S.: Resource utilization prediction technique in cloud using knowledge based ensemble random forest with lstm model. Concurrent Eng. **29**(4), 396–404 (2021)

23. Wang, M., Deng, W.: Deep visual domain adaptation: a survey. Neurocomputing **312**, 135–153 (2018)

24. Wu, Y., Liu, J., Wang, C., Xie, X., Shi, G.: Graph transformer and LSTM attention for VNF multi-step workload prediction in sfc. IEEE Trans. Netw. Service Manag. (2024)

25. Xi, H., Yan, C., Li, H., Xiao, Y.: An attention-based recurrent neural network for resource usage prediction in cloud data center. J. Phys. Conf. Ser. **2006**, 012007 (2021)

26. Yazdanian, P., Sharifian, S.: E2lg: a multiscale ensemble of lstm/gan deep learning architecture for multistep-ahead cloud workload prediction. J. Supercomput. **77**, 11052–11082 (2021)

27. Zhang, Q., Zhani, M.F., Zhang, S., Zhu, Q., Boutaba, R., Hellerstein, J.L.: Dynamic energy-aware capacity provisioning for cloud computing environments. In: Proceedings of the 9th International Conference on Autonomic Computing, pp. 145–154 (2012)

28. Zheng, H., et al.: Energy optimisation in cloud datacentres with mc-tide: mixed channel time-series dense encoder for workload forecasting. Appl. Energy **374**, 123903 (2024)

Enhancing Medical Data Management and Sharing with Blockchain Technology: A Focus on Encrypted NFTs

L. K. Bang[1], H. V. Khanh[1(✉)], M. N. Triet[1], N. N. Hung[1], P. D. Trinh[1], N. H. Bang[1], N. T. Anh[1], and K. T. N. Ngan[2]

[1] FPT University, Can Tho City, Vietnam
khanhvh@fe.edu.vn
[2] FPT Polytechnic, Can Tho City, Vietnam

Abstract. This paper explores the integration of blockchain technology in the management and sharing of medical data, specifically through the use of encrypted Non-Fungible Tokens (NFTs) and the InterPlanetary File System (IPFS). We address the traditional challenges of data security, privacy, and interoperability in healthcare systems by proposing a blockchain-based framework. Our study evaluates various encryption algorithms-RSA, RC4, DES, ChaCha20, Blowfish, and AES-to determine the most suitable for encrypting metadata associated with NFTs. Additionally, we analyze transaction fees across four Ethereum Virtual Machine (EVM)-compatible platforms-BNB Chain, Fantom, Polygon, and Celo-to assess their economic efficiency and suitability for healthcare applications. The research aims to demonstrate how blockchain technology can provide a secure, efficient, and transparent method for managing medical data, thus enhancing patient care and operational efficiency within healthcare systems.

Keywords: Blockchain · Transparency in managing and sharing medical data · Data Privacy and Security · Smart Contracts · Encrypted NFTs

1 Introduction

The management and sharing of medical data is a critical aspect of modern healthcare systems. Traditional methods often rely on centralized databases and manual processes, which pose significant challenges in terms of data security, privacy, and interoperability. These challenges can lead to data fragmentation, where patient information is dispersed across multiple systems and providers, making it difficult to compile a comprehensive medical history. Additionally, centralized databases are vulnerable to hacking and data breaches, potentially exposing sensitive patient information. Furthermore, the lack of interoperability between different healthcare systems due to incompatible formats and standards

Y. Wang and L.-J. Zhang (Eds.): CLOUD 2024, LNCS 15423, pp. 69–82, 2025.
https://doi.org/10.1007/978-3-031-77153-8_7

impedes smooth data exchange, while manual processes increase the likelihood of errors in data entry and management.

Blockchain technology has emerged as a promising solution to these challenges, offering a decentralized approach to data management that enhances security and privacy. Blockchain's inherent properties, such as immutability and decentralization, make it well-suited for managing sensitive information like medical records. By ensuring that data is stored in a distributed manner, blockchain minimizes the risk of data loss and unauthorized access. Furthermore, the use of smart contracts in blockchain systems can automate various processes, reducing the need for manual intervention and thereby decreasing the potential for human error.

Moreover, our research delves into the broader applications of blockchain in healthcare, emphasizing its potential to transform patient care and data management. Studies by Bang et al. highlight the integration of blockchain with the Internet of Healthcare Things (IoHT), using smart contracts to enhance patient data privacy and control [2]. Similarly, research by Son et al. and Le et al. explores the use of permissioned ledgers like Hyperledger Fabric to provide swift and secure access to patient data in emergency situations [8,15]. These studies illustrate the diverse ways in which blockchain technology can address existing challenges in healthcare informatics.

One of the innovative applications of blockchain technology in healthcare is the use of Non-Fungible Tokens (NFTs) to represent medical data. Encrypted NFTs can encapsulate patient records, ensuring that each record is unique, traceable, and secure. This approach not only enhances data integrity but also facilitates the management and sharing of medical data in a transparent manner. NFTs can be securely transferred between parties, ensuring that the ownership and authenticity of medical records are maintained throughout their lifecycle.

In our study, we evaluate the performance of various encryption algorithms in the context of a blockchain-based system for managing and sharing medical data using encrypted NFTs. The encryption of metadata associated with NFTs is crucial for maintaining the privacy and security of medical data. We examine six encryption methods-RSA, RC4, DES, ChaCha20, Blowfish, and AES-to identify the optimal balance between security and operational efficiency. This analysis is vital for sustaining the system's performance and reliability, especially when dealing with frequent and varied medical data transactions.

The assessment of transaction fees across different blockchain platforms is another critical aspect of our study. Transaction fees directly impact the operational costs and scalability of blockchain solutions. We conduct a comparative analysis of transaction fees on four Ethereum Virtual Machine (EVM)-compatible platforms: BNB Chain, Fantom, Polygon, and Celo. By examining the fee structures of these platforms, we aim to determine their economic efficiency and suitability for managing medical data. Our focus is on three essential operations: creating transactions, minting encrypted NFTs, and transferring these NFTs. These operations are fundamental to the lifecycle of medical data transactions on the blockchain.

Our evaluation highlights the need for a blockchain solution that provides the necessary functionality at minimal expense. The goal is to identify a platform that balances operational costs with system performance, thereby enhancing value for all stakeholders involved in the management and sharing of medical data. The findings from our analysis provide insights into the overall efficiency and cost-effectiveness of various blockchain networks, guiding the selection of the most suitable platform for establishing reliable and transparent medical data management systems.

In summary, our paper provides a comprehensive analysis of blockchain technology's role in enhancing the management and sharing of medical data through the use of encrypted NFTs and IPFS. By evaluating encryption algorithms and transaction fees, we aim to identify the most effective and efficient blockchain solutions for healthcare applications. Our findings contribute to the growing body of research on blockchain in healthcare, offering practical insights for the development of secure and transparent medical data management systems.

2   Related Work

2.1   Blockchain Applications in General Healthcare Systems

In healthcare informatics, the integration of blockchain technology is gaining prominence due to its potential to enhance systems that are centered around patient care. Research conducted by Bang et al. highlights the integration of blockchain with the Internet of Healthcare Things (IoHT), noting the use of smart contracts to bolster patient data privacy and control [2]. Additional studies by Son et al. and Le et al. have investigated the implementation of permissioned ledgers like Hyperledger Fabric, which are critical for providing swift and secure access to patient data in emergency situations [8,15].

The work of Duong et al. delves into how blockchain can foster more patient-oriented healthcare systems. Their research stresses the importance of maintaining data privacy and enhancing patient autonomy regarding their health records through the use of smart contracts [5,6]. Similarly, Wilber et al. have reviewed multiple applications of blockchain across healthcare, suggesting its broad potential to assist various facets of the industry, including patient care and pharmaceutical logistics [17].

Regarding electronic medical records (EMRs), De et al. and Madine et al. have proposed blockchain-based frameworks that ensure patients retain control over their information while enabling secure access for medical professionals [9, 10]. In an innovative approach, Shynu et al. have explored combining blockchain with fog computing to advance disease prediction methods, potentially enhancing data management and the efficacy of prognostic treatments [14].

2.2   Healthcare and Privacy Protection

Blockchain technology is increasingly recognized for its capacity to bolster data privacy and security within healthcare systems. Shi et al. conducted a comprehensive review on how blockchain technology can significantly enhance the security and privacy features of electronic health record (EHR) systems [13]. Kumar et al. underscored the necessity for healthcare frameworks that operate on a basis of transparency rather than trust, pointing out how blockchain can revolutionize the sector by facilitating clear agreements via smart contracts despite existing challenges [7]. Additionally, Tith et al. advocated for a consortium blockchain to interconnect various EHRs to boost privacy and enable secure, transparent access with immutable audit trails [16], while Chen et al. described how blockchain could secure the transmission, storage, and sharing of medical data through its inherent properties like immutability and decentralization [3].

In another application, Yue et al. introduced a blockchain-based system that allows patients to securely manage and share their healthcare data. This system utilizes an access model and schema to effectively organize personal healthcare data and employs Secure Multi-Party Computing (MPC) to ensure data privacy during processing [18]. These examples illustrate blockchain's potential to significantly improve security and privacy in healthcare data management.

Further research by Zhang, Xue, and Liu highlighted the importance of mitigating privacy and security risks in blockchain applications for medical data sharing. They suggest employing advanced technical measures like attribute-based encryption and zero-knowledge proofs to enhance data security [19]. Dagher et al. introduced "Ancile", a blockchain-based privacy-preserving framework that ensures the secure interoperability of electronic health records with robust access control implemented through smart contracts [4].

Continuing this theme, Vinnarasi A et al. discussed the use of permissioned blockchains integrated with the Internet of Things to protect healthcare data against unauthorized access while maintaining data integrity [1]. Parmar and Shah examined the combination of blockchain and cryptography to strengthen medical data security, thus aiding in compliance with data protection regulations [11]. Moreover, Ponsam, Duvvuri, and Roy detailed a blockchain system designed for efficient management of electronic health records, emphasizing data privacy, integrity, and interoperability among various healthcare providers [12]. Together, these studies demonstrate the evolving role of blockchain in addressing key challenges in healthcare data management (Fig. 1).

3   Approach

Traditional approaches to managing and sharing medical data typically depend on centralized databases and manual methods, which can result in various challenges. One significant issue is data fragmentation, where patient information is dispersed across multiple systems and providers, making it challenging to piece together a comprehensive medical history. Centralized databases also pose security risks, as they are susceptible to hacking and data breaches, potentially exposing sensitive patient information. Additionally, the lack of interoperability between different healthcare systems-owing to incompatible formats and standards-impedes smooth data exchange. Manual processes further exacerbate these problems by increasing the likelihood of errors in data entry and management.

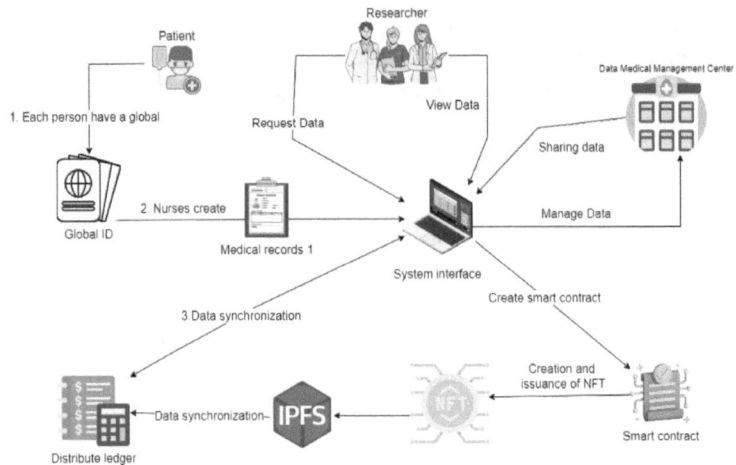

Fig. 1. Workflow of blockchain-based medical data management and sharing

The image 1 depicts a detailed framework for the management and exchange of medical data using blockchain and encrypted NFT technology. This model aims to resolve various issues and constraints that are commonly found in conventional medical data management and sharing practices.

Step 1. Assignment of Global ID: The initial step involves assigning a Global ID to each patient. This identifier is crucial for ensuring a consistent and traceable record of the patient's medical history. With a Global ID, patient data can be uniformly linked across different healthcare providers and systems, which aids in better coordination and continuity of care.

Step 2. Creation of Medical Records: When a patient visits a healthcare facility, nurses are responsible for creating and updating the patient's medical records. These records, referred to as "Medical records" in the diagram, include comprehensive details about the patient's medical history, treatments received, and ongoing care plans. Accurate and complete records are vital for effective patient management and informed decision-making.

Step 3. Data Synchronization: After creating the medical records, a data synchronization process is implemented to securely store and distribute this information using blockchain technology and the InterPlanetary File System (IPFS). Blockchain, due to its decentralized structure, enhances the security and integrity of the data. Using IPFS ensures that the data is stored in a distributed manner, minimizing the risk of data loss and enabling access from multiple locations as needed.

Step 4. Data Management and Sharing: The Data Medical Management Center is tasked with the management and sharing of medical data. When researchers or other authorized entities request access to medical data, these requests are processed through a system interface. Researchers can view the data after obtaining the necessary permissions, ensuring that only authorized individuals access sensitive medical information, thereby maintaining confidentiality and security.

Step 5. Smart Contracts and NFTs: To manage data access and security effectively, the system interface supports the creation of smart contracts. These contracts specify the terms and conditions for data access, providing clear guidelines on who can view and use the medical data. Additionally, the encrypted medical data is encapsulated into Non-Fungible Tokens (NFTs), which are created and issued as part of this process. NFTs serve as unique digital representations of the medical records, ensuring that each record is distinct and traceable, adding an extra layer of security to prevent unauthorized alterations or duplications.

Step 6. Distributed Ledger: The entire process, including the creation and access to smart contracts and encrypted NFTs, is recorded on a distributed ledger. This ledger maintains a transparent and immutable record of all transactions and access logs. The use of a distributed ledger ensures a permanent and auditable trail of data access and modifications, which is crucial for traceability and accountability in managing medical data.

Step 7. Enhanced Data Security and Integrity: Data synchronization between the system and IPFS supports the secure and distributed storage of medical records. By integrating blockchain and IPFS technologies, this model offers a comprehensive framework for managing and sharing medical data. It upholds high standards of security and data integrity, addressing challenges like data fragmentation, lack of interoperability, and vulnerability to data breaches. This method aims to provide a more reliable and secure approach to handling medical data, ensuring controlled and secure management and sharing.

4   Evaluation

4.1   Evaluation of Encrypted NFT Framework for Efficiency in Enhancing Transparency in Managing and Sharing Medical Data

In the Evaluation section of our study, we assess various encryption algorithms to bolster the security of metadata for Non-Fungible Tokens (NFTs) used in our blockchain-based system for managing and sharing medical data transparently. We scrutinize six encryption methods-RSA, RC4, DES, ChaCha20, Blowfish, and AES-to determine the optimal balance between security and operational efficiency. This analysis is vital for maintaining the system's performance and reliability. We focus on the encryption speed and security level of each algorithm, especially their capacity to safeguard encrypted NFTs and data stored on the InterPlanetary File System (IPFS). Our findings, which include performance metrics for encrypting text and image data, are crucial for upholding the integrity and transparency of medical data transactions, as outlined in our detailed tables.

The table presents performance metrics for RSA encryption across ten different trials, focusing on key generation, image encryption, and decryption, as well as text encryption and decryption. Key generation times vary widely, from as

Table 1. RSA Encryption and Decryption Performance for Image and text Data in Microseconds

RSA	1	2	3	4	5	6	7	8	9	10
Generating key	79703	136477	52146	53306	25536	78950	47233	40353	75905	98625
Encrypting image	13876	6599	14334	12974	10536	7130	6152	6704	10979	10646
Decrypting image	181893	185064	186860	178432	187234	184848	178727	190148	259331	260586
Generating key	56170	86070	101545	21061	111394	68302	279347	134955	46018	82341
Encrypting text	0	0	0	0	0	0	0	0	0	998
Decrypting text	0	1172	0	0	0	1084	0	0	502	0

low as 25,536 to as high as 279,347 microseconds, indicating significant fluctuation across trials. Image encryption times are generally lower, ranging from 6,130 to 14,334 microseconds, while image decryption times are substantially higher, often exceeding 178,000 microseconds, with two instances nearing or exceeding 260,000 microseconds. Interestingly, the times for encrypting and decrypting text are negligible or zero in most cases, except for a few instances where decryption times slightly exceed 1,000 microseconds. This data, summarized in the Table 1, highlights the robust security of RSA but also underscores its potential limitations in terms of computational efficiency, particularly when handling large data sets like images, which could impact the performance of blockchain systems used for managing medical data.

Table 2. RC4 Encryption and Decryption Performance for Image and text Data in Microseconds

RC4 (image)	1	2	3	4	5	6	7	8	9	10
Encrypting image	0	0	0	0	0	0	0	0	0	0
Decrypting image	0	0	0	0	0	0	0	0	0	0
Encrypting text	0	0	0	0	0	0	0	0	0	0
Decrypting text	0	0	0	0	0	0	0	0	0	0

The Table 2 provides a performance overview of RC4 encryption and decryption for both image and text data across ten trials, revealing an exceptionally fast processing time, with all operations completing in virtually zero microseconds. This speed highlights RC4's capability for quick data processing, which could be advantageous for enhancing transaction speeds within blockchain systems managing and sharing medical data. However, despite its efficiency, RC4's weaker security profile compared to more advanced encryption methods poses a significant dilemma. The choice between RC4's high speed and its lower security level is critical, especially in applications where maintaining high data integrity and security is paramount, mirroring similar trade-offs observed with the RSA algorithm's impact on system performance due to its slower operational speeds.

Table 3. DES Encryption and Decryption Performance for Image and text Data in Microseconds

DES (image)	1	2	3	4	5	6	7	8	9	10
Encrypting image	518	503	88	542	75	521	286	585	473	506
Decrypting image	12563	0	503	0	651	0	0	506	529	590
Encrypting text	0	0	0	0	0	0	0	0	0	0
Decrypting text	0	0	0	0	0	0	0	0	0	0

The Table 3 illustrates the performance metrics for DES encryption and decryption for image and text data across ten trials. For image data, encryption times were generally low, varying from 75 to 585 microseconds, with some trials showing notable outliers like 88 and 75 microseconds, suggesting quick processing capabilities. Decryption times for images, however, displayed more variability, with several trials recording zero microseconds, interspersed with times reaching up to 1,258 microseconds, indicating potential inconsistencies in processing speeds. Text data encryption and decryption were uniformly recorded at zero microseconds, highlighting extreme efficiency for smaller data sizes. Despite these favorable processing times, DES's known security vulnerabilities could undermine its suitability for securing medical data within a blockchain system, reflecting the ongoing challenge of balancing operational efficiency with robust security, similar to the trade-offs discussed with RC4 and RSA.

Table 4. Chacha20 Encryption and Decryption Performance for Image and text Data in Microseconds

CHACHA20 (image)	1	2	3	4	5	6	7	8	9	10
Encrypting image	544	0	0	519	0	0	0	518	83	0
Decrypting image	0	0	1503	0	0	0	0	0	0	0
Encrypting text	0	0	0	0	0	0	0	0	0	0
Decrypting text	0	0	0	0	0	0	0	0	0	0

The Table 4 outlines the performance of ChaCha20 encryption and decryption for both image and text data across ten trials, demonstrating its effective balance between speed and security. For image data, encryption times were generally very low, with several trials recording zero microseconds and others such as 544, 519, and 518 microseconds indicating fast processing capabilities. A notable exception was a single decryption trial that reached 1,503 microseconds, suggesting some variability in performance. However, the overwhelming majority of image decryption times, along with all encrypting and decrypting operations for text data, registered at zero microseconds, emphasizing ChaCha20's capacity for extremely quick data processing. This combination of rapid performance and robust security makes ChaCha20 a strong candidate for securing sensitive medical data within blockchain systems, presenting a significant improvement in both speed and security reliability compared to other evaluated algorithms like DES, RC4, and RSA.

Table 5. Blowfish Encryption and Decryption Performance for Image and text Data in Microseconds

blowfish (image)	1	2	3	4	5	6	7	8	9	10
Encrypting image	651	582	586	0	632	505	688	1137	633	541
Decrypting image	520	508	0	0	0	103	0	999	575	532
Encrypting text	0	0	0	0	0	0	91	0	0	0
Decrypting text	0	0	0	0	0	0	0	0	0	0

The Table 5 showcases the performance metrics of Blowfish encryption for image and text data across ten trials, highlighting its moderate efficiency in a blockchain system for managing medical data. Image encryption times varied, with results ranging from 0 to 1,137 microseconds, suggesting occasional rapid processing alongside higher times, which could impact system responsiveness. Decrypting image data also showed significant variation, with many trials showing zero microseconds, but others, like 999 microseconds, indicating potential delays in processing. Text data encryption and decryption consistently recorded zero microseconds, except for a single outlier in text encryption at 91 microseconds. Although Blowfish historically offered a good balance of speed and security, these results, combined with its aging algorithm against contemporary cybersecurity threats, suggest that it may no longer provide the optimal security required for sensitive medical data within modern blockchain systems, mirroring concerns similar to those observed with DES and other encryption standards like RC4, RSA, and ChaCha20.

Table 6. AES Encryption and Decryption Performance for Image and text Data in Microseconds

AES (image)	1	2	3	4	5	6	7	8	9	10
Encrypting image	0	0	633	82	0	0	0	541	557	503
Decrypting image	0	0	299	0	0	0	0	0	504	0
Encrypting text	0	0	0	0	0	0	0	0	0	0
Decrypting text	0	0	0	0	0	0	0	0	0	0

The Table 6 details the performance of AES encryption and decryption for both image and text data, illustrating its exceptional efficiency and reliability for a blockchain system managing medical data. For image data, encryption times are impressively low, with several instances at zero microseconds, and the highest recorded time being only 633 microseconds. Decryption times for images also demonstrate excellent speed, with most trials recording zero microseconds and the highest time peaking at just 504 microseconds. Both encrypting and decrypting text data consistently show zero microseconds across all trials, confirming the near-instantaneous processing capability of AES. This table underscores AES's superior performance in terms of both speed and reliability when compared to other algorithms like Blowfish, ChaCha20, and DES, reinforcing its suitability for safeguarding sensitive medical data while ensuring rapid access within the system.

The data we have gathered provides insights into the performance of various encryption algorithms within a blockchain-based system designed for managing and sharing medical data transparently. We are evaluating six encryption methods-RSA, RC4, DES, ChaCha20, Blowfish, and AES-to find an appropriate balance between security and operational efficiency. Our system, which utilizes smart contracts and encrypted NFTs to secure and manage medical records, requires an encryption strategy that can handle the dynamic nature of medical data transactions, characterized by frequent and varied interactions. Our comprehensive testing and analysis aim to select an encryption method that meets stringent security requirements while supporting the fast operational pace necessary for effective data management. This approach is crucial for maintaining a reliable and transparent system that secures the trust of users and stakeholders.

4.2   Testing on the Four EVM-Supported Platforms

Implementing blockchain technology in the management and sharing of medical data necessitates a careful evaluation of transaction fees, as these fees significantly impact the operational costs and scalability of blockchain solutions. This section offers a comparative analysis of transaction fees across four Ethereum Virtual Machine (EVM)-compatible platforms: BNB Chain, Fantom, Polygon, and Celo. We examine the fee structures of these platforms to determine their suitability for cost-effective blockchain-based systems for managing medical data, focusing on affordability and functionality in various operational scenarios.

Our study delves into enhancing medical data management and sharing through blockchain technology, integrating encrypted NFTs and IPFS within the system. The analysis centers on three essential functions: data creation, NFT minting, and NFT transfer. These processes are vital for recording transactions, validating data authenticity, and securely distributing digital assets among stakeholders.

In assessing the practicality and performance of these platforms, we specifically consider BNB Chain, Fantom, Celo, and Polygon. Each platform is evaluated for its ability to support the operations necessary for efficient management of medical data. Special attention is paid to the efficiency and cost-effectiveness of transaction processes, aiding in the identification of the most appropriate platforms for establishing reliable and transparent systems in medical data management and sharing.

4.3   Results

Evaluating transaction fees is essential when analyzing blockchain-based systems, particularly in the context of managing and sharing medical data. These fees are pivotal in determining the economic viability and sustainability of the system for all involved parties. They compensate validators or miners for securing the network and processing transactions.

Our analysis focuses on three critical operations vital to platforms managing medical data using encrypted NFTs: creating data/transactions, minting encrypted NFTs, and transferring these NFTs. Each operation plays a crucial role in the lifecycle of a medical data transaction on the blockchain:

1. Creation of Data or Transactions: This process involves documenting details about medical data transactions on the blockchain, ensuring that transaction details are permanently and transparently logged. The fees associated with this process are significant as they directly impact the cost to users for tokenizing their medical data.
2. Minting of Encrypted NFTs: This step transforms details of medical data transactions into unique digital assets-encrypted NFTs-that represent ownership or certification. This transformation is essential for the digital representation of medical data, facilitating its management. Evaluating the minting fees is crucial to keeping the process economical and accessible, thus supporting the efficient management of medical data.
3. Transferring Encrypted NFTs: This involves the change of ownership of digital assets between parties and is central to the functionality of the medical data management system. It enables the circulation and distribution of medical data credits. The costs linked to transferring encrypted NFTs affect the liquidity and ease of transactions within the system. High transfer fees might discourage frequent transactions and decrease system participation, whereas lower fees could encourage more active engagement.

By analyzing the fees associated with these key functions, we gain insights into the overall efficiency and cost-effectiveness of the blockchain platform for managing medical data. This analysis aids in comparing various blockchain networks to identify the most suitable platform based on a balance of operational costs and network performance. Our objective is to identify a blockchain solution that delivers the necessary functionality at minimal costs, optimizing benefits for all stakeholders in the medical data management ecosystem.

Transaction Fee Analysis. Table 7 presents a comparative analysis of transaction fees for three essential operations across four Ethereum Virtual Machine (EVM)-compatible blockchain platforms: BNB Chain, Fantom, Polygon, and

Table 7. Transaction fee

	Transaction Creation	Create NFT	Transfer NFT
BNB	0.0273134 BNB ($16.47)	0.00109162 BNB ($0.66)	0.00057003 BNB ($0.34)
Fantom	0.00957754 FTM ($0.00)	0.000405167 FTM ($0.00)	0.0002380105 FTM ($0.00)
Polygon	0.006840710032835408 MATIC ($0.01)	0.000289405001852192 MATIC ($0.00)	0.000170007501088048 MATIC ($0.00)
Celo	0.007097844 CELO ($0.005)	0.0002840812 CELO ($0.000)	0.0001554878 CELO ($0.000)

Celo, based on token prices as of May 27, 2024. These operations-creating transactions, minting encrypted NFTs, and transferring encrypted NFTs-are crucial for the management and protection of medical data using blockchain technology. By examining the fee structures of each platform, we can evaluate their economic efficiency and suitability for systems designed to manage and share medical data transparently using blockchain technology, encrypted NFTs, smart contracts, and IPFS.

The BNB Chain incurs a relatively higher fee for transaction creation, recorded at 0.0273134 BNB or approximately $16.47, which could impact the affordability of frequent transaction activities. In contrast, the fees for creating and transferring NFTs are significantly lower, at 0.00109162 BNB ($0.66) and 0.00057003 BNB ($0.34) respectively. This fee structure suggests that BNB Chain may be suitable for enterprises managing large volumes of medical data transactions represented as encrypted NFTs.

Fantom stands out with its exceptionally low fee structure, with a transaction creation fee of just 0.00957754 FTM. Additionally, the costs for minting and transferring NFTs are minimal, at 0.000405167 FTM and 0.0002380105 FTM respectively. This cost efficiency makes Fantom an appealing option for systems that require frequent updates and exchanges of encrypted NFTs representing medical data.

Polygon offers a nominal transaction creation fee of 0.006840710032835408 MATIC (approximately $0.01), along with very modest fees for NFT creation and transfer, set at 0.000289405001852192 MATIC and 0.000170007501088048 MATIC respectively. These low fees facilitate cost-effective scaling of operations, making it suitable for managing a wide range of medical data assets and promoting broader adoption and utilization of encrypted NFTs in the medical sector.

Celo focuses on mobile accessibility and affordability, charging a transaction creation fee of 0.007097844 CELO (around $0.005). Fees for NFT creation and transfer are even lower, at 0.0002840812 CELO and 0.0001554878 CELO respectively, making them almost negligible in cost. This pricing model is particularly advantageous for participants in regions with limited financial resources, supporting the development of efficient medical data management systems.

By evaluating these transaction fees, we gain valuable insights into the efficiency and economic viability of various blockchain platforms for managing medical data. This evaluation enables us to compare different networks and identify the most suitable platform by balancing operational costs against system performance. Our objective is to find a blockchain solution that provides the necessary functionality at minimal expense, thereby enhancing value for all stakeholders involved in the transparent management and sharing of medical data utilizing blockchain Encrypted NFTs.

5   Conclusion

The findings from our research indicate that blockchain technology, when coupled with encrypted NFTs and IPFS, offers a robust solution to the challenges of managing and sharing medical data. The deployment of smart contracts and blockchain's inherent properties such as decentralization and immutability significantly enhance data security and privacy. Our evaluation of encryption algorithms reveals that while there is no one-size-fits-all solution, certain algorithms provide a favorable balance between security and efficiency, suitable for the dynamic nature of medical data. The analysis of transaction fees further supports the feasibility of adopting blockchain technology, with certain platforms showing greater economic efficiency and operational effectiveness for medical data management.

This study contributes to the evolving field of healthcare informatics by providing a detailed analysis of how blockchain technology can be leveraged to improve the management and sharing of medical data. The implementation of such systems could potentially transform patient care by ensuring data integrity, security, and accessibility. Future research should continue to explore the integration of advanced cryptographic techniques and the expansion of blockchain applications in other areas of healthcare to fully realize the technology's potential in this critical sector.

References

1. A, P.V., Dayana, R., Vadivukkarasi, K.: Healthcare data security using blockchain technology. In: 2023 International Conference on Intelligent Systems for Communication, IoT and Security (ICISCoIS) (2023)
2. Bang, N., et al.: Blockchain-enhanced ioht: a patient-centric internet of healthcare things platform with smart contract-driven data management. In: International Conference on Advances in Mobile Computing and Multimedia Intelligence, pp. 50–56. Springer (2023). https://doi.org/10.1007/978-3-031-48348-6_4
3. Chen, Z., et al.: A blockchain-based preserving and sharing system for medical data privacy. Futur. Gener. Comput. Syst. **124**, 338–350 (2021)
4. Dagher, G.G., Mohler, J., Milojkovic, M., Marella, P.B.: Ancile: privacy-preserving framework for access control and interoperability of electronic health records using blockchain technology. Sustainable Cities Soc. (2018)

5. Duong-Trung, N., et al.: On components of a patient-centered healthcare system using smart contract. In: Proceedings of the 2020 4th International Conference on Cryptography, Security and Privacy, pp. 31–35 (2020)
6. Duong-Trung, N., et al.: Smart care: integrating blockchain technology into the design of patient-centered healthcare systems. In: Proceedings of the 2020 4th International Conference on Cryptography, Security and Privacy, pp. 105–109 (2020)
7. Kumar, T., Ramani, V., Ahmad, I., Braeken, A., Harjula, E., Ylianttila, M.: Blockchain utilization in healthcare: key requirements and challenges. In: 2018 IEEE 20th International Conference on e-Health Networking, Applications and Services (Healthcom), pp. 1–7. IEEE (2018)
8. Le, H.T., et al.: Patient-chain: patient-centered healthcare system a blockchain-based technology in dealing with emergencies. In: Shen, H., et al. (eds.) PDCAT 2021. LNCS, vol. 13148, pp. 576–583. Springer, Cham (2022). https://doi.org/10.1007/978-3-030-96772-7_54
9. Madine, M.M., et al.: Blockchain for giving patients control over their medical records. IEEE Access 8, 193102–193115 (2020)
10. de Oliveira, M.T., et al.: Towards a blockchain-based secure electronic medical record for healthcare applications. In: ICC 2019-2019 IEEE International Conference on Communications (ICC), pp. 1–6. IEEE (2019)
11. Parmar, M., Shah, S.: Reinforcing security of medical data using blockchain. In: 2019 International Conference on Intelligent Computing and Control Systems (ICCS) (2019)
12. Ponsam, D.J.G., Duvvuri, S., Roy, S.: Electronic healthcare management system using blockchain technology. In: 2023 International Conference on Circuit Power and Computing Technologies (ICCPCT) (2023)
13. Shi, S., et al.: Applications of blockchain in ensuring the security and privacy of electronic health record systems: a survey. Comput. Sec. 97, 101966 (2020)
14. Shynu, P., et al.: Blockchain-based secure healthcare application for diabetic-cardio disease prediction in fog computing. IEEE Access 9, 45706–45720 (2021)
15. Son, H.X., Le, T.H., Quynh, N.T.T., Huy, H.N.D., Duong-Trung, N., Luong, H.H.: Toward a blockchain-based technology in dealing with emergencies in patient-centered healthcare systems. In: Bouzefrane, S., Laurent, M., Boumerdassi, S., Renault, E. (eds.) MSPN 2020. LNCS, vol. 12605, pp. 44–56. Springer, Cham (2021). https://doi.org/10.1007/978-3-030-67550-9_4
16. Tith, D., et al.: Application of blockchain to maintaining patient records in electronic health record for enhanced privacy, scalability, and availability. Healthcare Inform. Res. 26(1), 3–12 (2020)
17. Wilber, K., et al.: A survey on blockchain for healthcare informatics and applications. In: 2020 7th International Conference on Internet of Things: Systems, Management and Security (IOTSMS), pp. 1–9. IEEE (2020)
18. Yue, X., et al.: Healthcare data gateways: found healthcare intelligence on blockchain with novel privacy risk control. J. Med. Syst. 40(10), 1–8 (2016)
19. Zhang, R., Xue, R., Liu, L.: Security and privacy for healthcare blockchains. IEEE Trans. Serv. Comput. (2021)

Innovation in the Digital Cultural Industry Within the Metaverse from the Perspectives of Physical and Virtual Mobility

Xinyi Lin[(✉)] and Xianying Chen

Communication University of China, Beijing 100024, CN, China
`xinyilin@cuc.edu.cn`

Abstract. The digital cultural industry integrates digital technology and network communication technology, playing a crucial role in the development of China's cultural industry and digital economy. Since 2020, the metaverse has become a vibrant arena for global technology companies and venture capital, significantly boosting the development of the digital economy and shaping the future of the cultural industry. Mobility theory, as an increasingly common academic perspective, provides a theoretical bridge for interdisciplinary research between the metaverse and the digital cultural industry. Following historical traces and analyzing the evolution and current trends of mobility theory, this paper identifies two aspects of mobility: physical and virtual. Physically, such as the movement of people in cultural spaces, and the flow of cultural data and cultural memory; virtually, such as the flow of cultural ideas and aesthetics, and the mobility of human-machine ethics. Based on this, the paper proposes the following development ideas: establishing a new model for nurturing digital nomads; creating a system for the rights and circulation of cultural data; and enacting policies to guide the construction of digital cultural communities and the cultivation of digital cultural values.

Keywords: Digital cultural industry · Mobility · Metaverse · Policy implications

1 Introduction

The digital culture industry is a new industry form that emerges from the deep integration of the cultural industry and the digital economy. It can be categorized into four main types: digital cultural technology and equipment manufacturing, digital creative content, digital cultural entertainment, and digital cultural services (Xu Yanping, Yue Qiang, 2024; Xiang Yong, 2022). As a core component of the digital economy, the digital culture industry has become a key direction for the development of China's cultural industry in the digital age. Exploring the development pathways of the digital culture industry is an urgent task in the new era. The report of the 20th National Congress of the Communist Party of China emphasizes the need to "promote the integrated cluster development of strategic emerging industries, and build new growth engines such as new-generation information technology, artificial intelligence, biotechnology, new energy, new materials, high-end equipment, and green and environmental protection technologies." The metaverse, as a comprehensive application of new-generation information technology, holds great potential for future development. Guided by the 20th National Congress, the Ministry of Industry and Information Technology, the Ministry of Education, the Ministry of Culture and Tourism, the State-owned Assets Supervision and Administration Commission of the State Council, and the General Office of the National Radio and Television Administration jointly issued the "Three-Year Action Plan for the Innovative Development of the Metaverse Industry (2023–2025)" in 2023, emphasizing the construction of advanced metaverse technology and industry systems. In the 11th collective study session of the Political Bureau of the CPC Central Committee, Xi Jinping emphasized that "developing new productive forces is an intrinsic requirement and an important focus for promoting high-quality development. We must continue to advance innovation and accelerate the development of new productive forces." It is foreseeable that metaverse technology will deeply influence China's digital economy and cultural industry in the future. Facing the burgeoning development of the digital culture industry and the metaverse, this article focuses on exploring their relationship and analyzing how the metaverse will reshape the fundamental forms of the digital culture industry.

Currently, literature on the digital culture industry primarily focuses on exploring its development pathways and regional economic benefits. For instance, Xu Yanping and Yue Qiang (2024) argue that to achieve high-quality development in the digital culture industry, it is essential to center on digital cultural construction by enhancing the digitalization of cultural production, accelerating the establishment of cultural industry technology standards, and building high-level cultural platforms to promote the sustainable development of the digital culture industry. However, the impact of the emerging metaverse on the digital culture industry has not yet attracted widespread attention from scholars. As an emerging concept after 2020, existing literature on the metaverse primarily focuses on exploring its definition. For example, Yu Guoming (2021) and others view the metaverse as "a real-time online world evolved from the internet, a

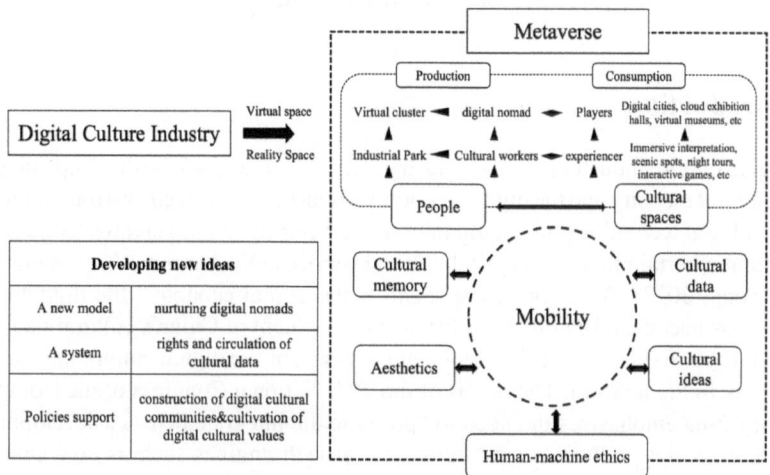

Fig. 1. The Mobility of Digital Cultural Industries in the Metaverse

new economic, social, and civilizational system composed of interconnected platforms across both online and offline spaces." Xiang Yong (2023) considers the metaverse to be a diverse world that constitutes people's living space, transcending the interaction between the real and virtual worlds. Building on existing research, this article explores the sustainable development pathways of the digital culture industry in the context of the metaverse, providing a new perspective for the study of the digital culture industry's development paths (see Fig. 1).

2   Literature Review

2.1   Conceptual Definition:Metaverse-Related Concepts in the Digital Culture Industry

In the digital culture industry, metaverse-related concepts are primarily based on four fundamentals: Digital Assets, Virtual Social Interaction, User-Generated Content (UGC), and AI-Generated Content (AIGC). The first is Digital Assets, which refers to any text or media items (including usage rights) stored on computers, smartphones, digital media, or in the cloud. Examples include digital currencies, NFTs, virtual real estate, digital artworks, virtual goods and clothing, digital music and e-books, in-game props and currencies, etc., which are valuable assets existing in electronic form that can be created, traded, distributed, and owned by metaverse users. The second is Virtual Social Interaction, where users engage in community building within a shared virtual space, exploring new forms of sociality in a digital environment. The third is User-Generated Content, which refers to content created by users, such as videos, images, and other forms of media. With blockchain technology, data security and objectivity can be ensured. The fourth is AI-Generated Content, where humans input text, images, videos, etc., into a computer, which then responds using a network database. Humans refine the final media content through prompts. Current notable industry applications include text-to-text (ChatGPT, Tongyi), text-to-image (Midjourney), and text-to-video (Pika), among others.

2.2   Theoretical basis:The Evolution of Mobility Theory

"Mobility" is a term with different meanings across various disciplines. From the perspective of English definitions, mobility is divided into "Liquidity," which pertains to economics and finance, and "Mobility," which relates to socio-economics, geographical movement and migration, and the field of information technology. The former relies on the Liquidity Hypothesis proposed by Coase (1937) in the theory of transaction costs, which suggests that there are certain costs associated with the price mechanism in organizing transactions. The rapid execution of trade orders can reduce transaction costs and ensure that trading activities do not impact market prices. In other words, liquidity is an important indicator of market efficiency and financial stability, and it is negatively correlated with transaction costs. The latter meaning of "Mobility" encompasses a broader range and is closely connected to political, economic, and social development. Mobility in this perspective existed as early as the slave society and manifested differently in different periods, becoming one of the driving forces of human social progress. The mobility discussed in this article falls under the category of "Mobility."

In ancient times, the mobility generated by the opening of new markets allowed merchants and skilled workers to maximize their income, though it was influenced by seasons and extreme weather (Funoon Al-Hamedi, 2023), and cultural mobility was not significant. From the 1950s to the 1980s, mobility did not originate from individual goals but was seen (by socialist countries) as a tool for economic and political development, such as in the mobility system connecting Eastern Europe with the Far East and Africa, where group movements were represented by students and labor migrants (mainly from Cuba, Vietnam, and Mozambique) from newly decolonized countries (Alena K. Alamgir, 2023). In the context of the fall of the Berlin Wall and globalization in the 1990s, the lower classes, when faced with class oppression, were more inclined to migrate to other regions rather than resorting to violent revolution. "Mobility" gradually replaced "revolution" as one of the driving forces of history, but at the same time, it became a label for the lower classes (Z Weng, 2022). It can be said that from early modern Europe to the contemporary era, the semantic overview of the concept of "Mobility" has gradually become more open and inclusive, and it is now considered a historical and social phenomenon that transcends local perspectives, playing a role in shaping society. Both the Frankfurt School and the Birmingham School have applied the concept of "Mobility" in their respective fields. Although the Frankfurt School did not incorporate mobility as a central theme in their works, it can still be metaphorically identified in their critiques of social structure and cultural reproduction, such as Max Horkheimer attributing the potential for individuals to move between social classes or challenge mainstream ideology to "a form of intellectual or ideological mobility." The Birmingham School more directly revealed the state of mobility within popular culture, focusing on the material development in communication studies. For example, Stuart Hall recognized the widespread nature of mobility in social structure, identity, and cultural communication. In 1985, Leo Bersani (a prominent figure in the study of sexuality, art, and culture) formally introduced the concept of "Mobility" in his anthology *The Forms of Violence*, which focused on ancient Assyrian narrative sculpture and applied the concept of "Mobility" from the field of visual analysis, indicating that mobility can bridge the gap between art and physics (Whitney Davis, 2022).

From the perspective of mobility, "Second Modernity" (Ulrich Beck, 2008), "Reflexive Modernity" (Anthony Giddens, 1998), and "Liquid Modernity" (Bauman, Z, 2013) all acknowledge that time and space are key dimensions of mobility. The "Spaces of Flows" theory suggests that spatial mobility has become a personal experience in the era of globalization, and the formation of new spatial logic does not mean that space becomes "placeless," but rather connects places with spaces (Manuel Castells, 1997). Later scholars further deconstructed the social significance of the mobility of people, objects, and ideas, and identified five interdependent systems and experiences of mobility: corporeal travel, the circulation of objects, imaginative travel, virtual travel, and communicative travel (Urry & Sheller, 2006).

With the expansion and transformation of theoretical frameworks and practical spaces, mobility has become an important research perspective in fields such as geography and anthropology. In the field of communication studies, scholars focus on the interactive relationship between the movement of media and elements. For example, David Morley, a representative figure in British media and cultural studies, elaborates on a mobility paradigm that transcends "media centrism" in his book *Communications and Mobility: The Migrant, the Mobile Phone, and the Container Box*, illustrating how various elements have acquired mobility attributes driven by new media. Additionally, some scholars have incorporated mobility into the definition of culture, viewing culture as a transnational "imaginary landscape" constructed based on global cultural flows (Arjun Appadurai, 2010).

It can be said that most scholars have expressed their understanding of "Mobility" from the perspectives of transportation displacement, population, migration, data, information technology, jobs and professions, residence, elderly travel, etc., with more attention given to the mobility of "physical elements," while the mobility of "virtual elements," such as collective memory, knowledge, and education, has been overlooked. This article argues that in addition to the spatial mobility of real elements like population, knowledge, information, and technology, there is also the mobility of virtual elements in the development of cultural society, such as cultural interaction and human-machine ethics.

Based on a historical review of the mobility paradigm, this article explores the current modes of mobility presented in the digital culture industry, including the mobility of people and scenes within cultural spaces, the mobility of cultural data and cultural memory, as well as the mobility of cultural concepts and cultural aesthetics, and human-machine ethics (mobility of virtual elements). In doing so, it refines the theory of mobility and examines the existence of cultural mobility within the metaverse.

3 Research Methods

3.1 Research Design

This study adopts a qualitative research methodology, integrating a comprehensive literature review with theoretical analysis to explore the relationship between the metaverse and the digital cultural industry from the perspective of mobility theory. The primary goal is to identify new developmental pathways for the digital cultural industry by examining both physical and virtual aspects of mobility within the metaverse context.

3.2 Data Collection

A systematic literature review was conducted to gather relevant academic articles, books, policy documents, and industry reports. The literature search spanned publications from 2000 to 2024 to capture both foundational theories and recent developments. Databases such as Web of Science, Scopus, Google Scholar, and China National Knowledge Infrastructure (CNKI) were utilized. Keywords used in the search included "digital cultural industry," "metaverse," "mobility theory," "cultural mobility," "digital nomads," "virtual clusters," "cultural data circulation," and "human-machine ethics."

3.3 Inclusion and Exclusion Criteria

The selection of literature was guided by the following criteria:
Inclusion Criteria:
Peer-reviewed articles, conference proceedings, authoritative reports, and policy documents.
Works focusing on the metaverse, digital cultural industry, or mobility theory.
Studies offering theoretical or empirical insights into cultural mobility in the digital era.
Exclusion Criteria:
Publications not available in full text.
Works unrelated to the core themes of this study.
Articles lacking rigorous academic standards or empirical support.

3.4 Data Analysis

The collected literature was analyzed using thematic analysis to identify key themes and patterns related to mobility in the digital cultural industry and the metaverse. The analysis involved:
Thematic Coding: Identifying recurrent themes such as physical mobility (movement of people and cultural spaces) and virtual mobility (flow of cultural concepts and ethics).
Content Analysis: Examining the content of selected works to understand how mobility theory has evolved and how it applies to the metaverse and digital culture.
Comparative Analysis: Comparing different scholarly perspectives to synthesize a cohesive understanding of mobility in the metaverse context.

3.5 Theoretical Framework Application

Mobility theory serves as the foundational theoretical framework for this study. By dissecting its historical evolution and current applications, the research:
Explores Physical Mobility: Investigates the movement of cultural producers (digital nomads) and the transformation of cultural spaces into virtual clusters.
Examines Virtual Mobility: Analyzes the flow of cultural data, memory, concepts, aesthetics, and the dynamics of human-machine ethics within the metaverse.

3.6 Validity and Reliability Measures

To ensure the credibility of the research:
Triangulation: Multiple data sources and perspectives were used to validate findings.
Expert Consultation: Insights were sought from scholars in cultural studies, communication, sociology, and information technology to verify interpretations.
Peer Review: Drafts were reviewed by peers to identify potential biases and improve analytical rigor.

3.7 Limitations

While the study provides comprehensive insights, it is constrained by:

Scope of Literature: Limited to available publications up to 2024, potentially missing the most recent developments.

Language Bias: Predominantly includes literature in English and Chinese, which may exclude relevant studies in other languages.

4 Results:Digital Cultural Mobility Patterns from the Perspective of the Metaverse

4.1 The Mobility of People and Scenes in Cultural Spaces

The mobility of people refers to the cross-regional movement of cultural producers and the shift of cultural industry clusters from the real to the virtual. This mobility is a key element of cultural evolution, enabling the formation of cultural hubs through industrial clustering that brings together entities for collaborative production. In recent years, with the significant enhancement of the transferability of cultural content, information resources, and data capital, cultural workers have begun to extend cultural production and services beyond fixed office locations to communities and rural areas, moving across regions. This trend, brought about by technological innovation, is referred to in sociology as the digital nomad phenomenon or the "digital nomad movement".

According to the "China Digital Nomad Survival Report (2023)", there are currently over "500,000 digital nomads" in China, dispersed both domestically and internationally. They participate in the production of the digital cultural industry through remote work and online collaboration. These digital nomads encompass designers, writers, musicians, game developers, and other professionals. Their mobility breaks regional limitations and injects new vitality into the digital cultural industry. By leveraging digital technology and data capital, and powered by new productive forces such as artificial intelligence, they carry, store, produce, sell, and circulate cultural content within the "third space" of the metaverse.

The mobility of scenes can be divided into the mobility of "cultural production scenes" and "cultural consumption scenes" (see Fig. 2).

"Cultural Production Scenes Mobility" is reflected in the shift of cultural industry parks towards the construction of virtual clusters. For example, "Shanghai's Zhangjiang Digital Cultural Industry Park" utilizes VR and AR technologies to construct an online virtual park, attracting digital cultural enterprises from around the globe. This creates a cross-regional industrial cluster effect, enabling collaboration and innovation without the constraints of physical location. Such virtual clusters allow enterprises to achieve remote editing and collaboration through network servers and cloud software, enhancing efficiency and fostering innovation.

In previous research, Xiang Yong (2016) categorized the factors behind the formation of Chinese cultural industry park clusters into social models, economic models, government models, and multi-faceted models. Industrial clustering is a development model jointly recognized by economics and geography for emerging industries. This approach

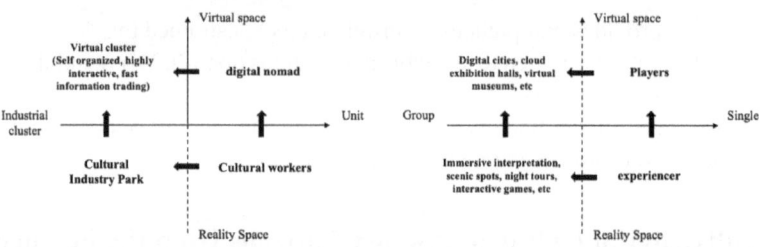

Fig. 2. Mobilty Forms of People and Scenes in the Production Consumption of Digital Culture Industry from the Perspective of Metaverse(2024)

is similarly projected into the construction of digital cities, leading to the management of virtual clusters by cultural industry parks.

"Cultural Consumption Scenes Mobility" is manifested in fully immersive presentation and interactive consumption spaces, which can be divided into real consumption spaces and virtual consumption spaces.

"Real Consumption Spaces" include cultural scenes and activities such as immersive performances, scenic spots, night tours, and interactive games that incorporate digital technology.

"Virtual Consumption Spaces" refer to digital cities, digital parks, cloud exhibition halls, virtual museums, and similar venues.

A prime example is the "Digital Palace Museum project" by the Palace Museum, which employs virtual reality technology to allow global audiences to visit the museum online and experience the charm of traditional Chinese culture. According to statistics, the "Digital Palace Museum" attracted over "10 million visits" in its first year of launch, significantly enhancing the convenience and enjoyment of cultural consumption. This project not only preserves cultural heritage through digital means but also broadens access to it, allowing users worldwide to engage with Chinese culture interactively.

It can be said that the current development of the metaverse is transforming cultural consumption into a "mobile experience", with the real and virtual gradually converging. The digital cultural "third space" it forms aligns more closely with the "people-oriented" concept, emphasizing the balance between real life and the virtual world.

4.2 The Mobility of Cultural Data and Cultural Memory

The mobility of cultural data is reflected in the reproduction and value enhancement of cultural big data.Under the guidance of national cultural big data and within the context of new productive forces, China has already laid out the digitization, storage, and protection of past cultural resources (including text, voice, books, music, calligraphy, animation, and movements). In the current digital era, the development of the cultural industry has seen production factors such as technology, creativity, and data permeating the entire process of cultural production. This has led to reduced marginal costs of industrial linkage and a tendency toward diversification of property rights (Shuyu Qi, 2023).

Case Study: The "Digital Dunhuang" Project. An exemplary illustration of cultural data mobility is the "Digital Dunhuang" project. By employing high-precision digital scanning and rendering technologies, the project has digitally preserved and showcased the Dunhuang frescoes. As of the end of 2023, the "Digital Dunhuang" platform has garnered over 20 million global visits, with users spanning more than 190 countries and regions. This project not only protects precious cultural heritage but also enables its widespread dissemination and reuse through digital means. The cultural elements (knowledge, information, images, videos, etc.) in virtual and real spaces "convert and produce" each other, forming a new way of regenerating cultural data. Elements nurtured in virtual spaces are seamlessly connected to the real world through advanced technologies such as VR, AR, and MR, and vice versa. This virtual-real interaction production model is of great significance for the creative transformation and innovative development of outstanding Chinese traditional culture in the new era.

Case Study: Industrial Application of Cultural Data—Alibaba's "Cultural Brain". Another example is Alibaba's "Cultural Brain" project, which utilizes big data and artificial intelligence technologies to analyze and mine cultural data, generating new cultural products and services. By analyzing user behavior, the system recommends personalized cultural content, enhancing user experience. This application demonstrates how the mobility of cultural data leads to its reproduction and value addition, contributing to the growth of the digital cultural industry.

The mobility of cultural memory mainly refers to the subject-object mobility generated by storing cultural memory in virtual digital humans. Memory is a crucial link in cultural connections between people and is key to passing down history and maintaining community identity. Henry Jenkins' concept of "participatory culture" explains how the "collective memory" of netizens has become part of popular culture, participating in the process of social construction.

Case Study: Virtual Digital Human "Ling". OA prominent example is Tencent's virtual idol "Ling". Not only does "Ling" possess a realistic appearance and movements, but she can also simulate human emotions and memories through machine learning. She has participated in the creation of multiple digital cultural works, such as virtual concerts and digital animations, becoming a carrier of cultural memory and attracting significant attention and engagement from young users. As a central figure in the metaverse, virtual digital humans like "Ling" bear the important responsibility of carrying cultural memory and have the potential to shape future popular culture.

In 2021, Professor Cai Wei's team at The Chinese University of Hong Kong (Shenzhen) established a conceptual model and information framework for digital memory in virtual digital humans, termed "Memory Digital Humans". This model includes five interconnected components: individual, family, field, culture, and interaction. It supports cultural memory institutions in constructing and preserving digital memory within the metaverse for long-term humanities and social science research.

4.3 The Mobility of Cultural Concepts and Cultural Aesthetics

The mobility of cultural concepts is embodied in the fusion of cyber culture and metaverse culture. Cyberpunk culture originated from the concept of "cyberspace" in the

Canadian science fiction novel Neuromancer (Gibson, 1984), depicting a world defined by computers, where matter and code coexist. In the era of underdeveloped media technology, cyber culture remained a marginal subculture, with symbols like hackers, NASA, computer companies, and military institutions primarily appearing in artistic works and not attracting widespread discussion. With the advancement of network technology and the introduction of the metaverse concept, virtualization, immersion, and spatiality have become central to the cultural agenda. Concepts like "cyberspace" and "cybertourism" illustrate how cyber culture, cyberspace, virtual reality, and digitization have formed a mutually embedded cultural whole. In this context, literature, art, development concepts, and consciousness have become unconsciously "Cyberized."

A prominent example of the fusion of cyber culture and metaverse culture is the open-world game "Genshin Impact" developed by miHoYo. This game combines cyber culture with elements of traditional Chinese culture to construct a virtual metaverse world. As of early 2024, "Genshin Impact" has achieved over 100 million cumulative global downloads, becoming a successful example of Chinese digital cultural products going global. The game seamlessly integrates cutting-edge digital technology with Chinese mythology, landscapes, and cultural symbols, allowing players worldwide to experience a unique blend of Eastern and Western cultural elements within a cyberized virtual environment. This not only enhances cultural exchange but also demonstrates the mobility of cultural concepts across different contexts.

Within the metaverse, users often emphasize intellectual property attributes, choosing culturally related identities with shared interests. They stress the principle of decentralization during collaboration—utilizing technologies such as blockchain and smart contracts—to ensure fairness and transparency. This metaverse culture carries the genes of cyber culture but moves away from individual resistance and anti-authoritarian revolutionary methods, focusing more on overall collaboration and rational decision-making.

The mobility of cultural aesthetics is the visualized presentation of the mobility of cultural concepts and represents a higher-level requirement for the digital cultural industry. The aesthetic value of the metaverse is a crucial part of its spiritual value, specifically reflected in the styles and visual effects in metaverse works, platforms, applications, and spaces.

An illustrative case is the Chinese aesthetics showcased in the "Digital Palace Museum." Through high-precision digitization of the Palace Museum's architecture and cultural relics, combined with virtual reality technology, the essence of Chinese culture is recreated. Users can closely view masterpieces like "Along the River During the Qingming Festival" in virtual space and experience urban life during the Song Dynasty. This innovative cultural experience enhances the public's understanding and appreciation of Chinese aesthetics, demonstrating how digital technology can bring traditional culture to life in immersive ways. By providing an interactive platform, the "Digital Palace Museum" has significantly increased public engagement with cultural heritage, making it accessible to a global audience.

From a macro perspective, the development trajectory of metaverse art styles can be divided into different stages: primary, intermediate, and advanced. Currently, it is in the primary stage, characterized by initial construction and exhibiting three art styles:

Cyber Aesthetic: Features urban sensibility, technological landscapes, neon lights, dark tones, metallic textures, and industrial styles, regarded as the initial imagination of the metaverse.

Hyperrealism Aesthetic: Excels in image detail richness, color fidelity, light and shadow contrast, and sharpness, represented by the text-to-video technology "Sora," released by OpenAI on February 15, 2024.

Post-Digital Aesthetic: Abnormal and abstract, similar to glitch art, commonly seen in digital artists' works.

Under the AIGC-dominated cultural production logic, new art styles are produced, disseminated, and transformed, placing popular culture in a state of "mobility" and "stability," leading to changes in aesthetic dimensions. The exploration of visual cultural thought reveals the metaphorical discourse behind the construction of visual culture. While AIGC imagery based on Western databases provides mass entertainment, it may also guide mass aesthetics into the framework of Western aesthetics, potentially reducing the perception of the harmony, artistic conception, and spirit of "Chinese imagery aesthetics."

In response, there is a growing emphasis on promoting and disseminating Chinese aesthetics within the metaverse. The proposition of beauty in imagery essentially restores the dominant role of the creative "heart" in aesthetic activities, driving the upgrade of beauty through imitation, simulation, and creation. The metaverse raises higher demands for the digital cultural industry, namely the transmission of beauty rooted in cultural heritage.

An example of this focus is CGTN's "Art Promotion Plan," which launched the digital exhibition "Millennium Tune: Song Dynasty Landscapes and Flowers." Through six thematic web pages, the exhibition produced 22 interview videos with domestic and foreign experts and featured 156 high-definition images of Song Dynasty paintings. This initiative deeply analyzes the realistic techniques, spiritual connotations, and humanistic values of Chinese masterpieces such as "Travelers Among Mountains and Streams," "Early Spring," "Layered Mountains on Misty River," and "A Recluse's Tour of the Xiao and Xiang Rivers." By adhering to cultural and value stances, the project focuses on transmitting cultural values centered on beauty, enhancing global appreciation for Chinese art.

In the context of globalization, there is enhanced cultural confidence and a growing demand to promote and disseminate Chinese aesthetics. The desire to share cultural heritage and values internationally propels the mobility of cultural concepts and aesthetics.The advancement of digital technology and deepening international cultural exchanges facilitate this mobility. Technologies like VR, AR, and digital rendering enable immersive cultural experiences, while global platforms allow for widespread dissemination. These initiatives have promoted the international dissemination of Chinese culture and enhanced the soft power of the cultural industry. By integrating traditional aesthetics with modern technology, they contribute to cultural diversity within the metaverse and offer new avenues for cultural innovation.

4.4   The Mobility of Human-Machine Ethics

The mobility of human-machine ethics is manifested as the internal mobility between humans and artificial intelligence, encompassing aspects such as appearances, thoughts, emotions, and morals. This "mobility" in the process of human-machine interaction is projected into virtual space in a "network topological" structure, further participating in cultural development and exerting a profound impact on cultural mobility.

From the perspective of species relativism, there is "moral continuity" between humans and animals, suggesting that non-human species also possess inherent behavioral norms and moral possibilities—including altruism, reciprocity, trust, punishment, sympathy, compassion, care, help, competition, sharing, and a desire for fairness. These individual moral and behavioral habits are being replicated into the moral continuity between humans and machines. The development of the metaverse, based on existing social structures and divisions of labor, will further explore the possibilities of future social structures and governance in a progressive and evolving manner, influencing the development of the digital cultural industry.

Case Study: Emotional Interaction with Microsoft's Xiaoice.   An illustrative example of the mobility of human-machine ethics is the emotional interaction enabled by Microsoft's AI, "Xiaoice." Having evolved to its eighth generation, Xiaoice is capable of engaging in emotional dialogues, poetry creation, music composition, and more. According to data, as of 2023, Xiaoice has interacted with over 660 million users and has created over 100 million poems. This extensive interaction not only showcases the advanced capabilities of AI in simulating human-like emotions and creativity but also raises significant discussions on issues such as the copyright of AI-generated creations, the nature of human-machine relationships, and the ethical considerations involved.

Xiaoice's ability to compose poetry and music blurs the lines between human and machine creativity, challenging traditional notions of authorship and intellectual property rights. For instance, who holds the copyright to a poem written by an AI? Additionally, as users form emotional connections with Xiaoice, questions arise about the psychological impact of such relationships and the responsibilities of developers in managing user interactions with AI. The emotional bonds formed between users and AI entities necessitate careful consideration of ethical guidelines to protect users from potential psychological harm.

Case Study: The Rise of Virtual Anchors.   Another example is the emergence of virtual anchors on live streaming platforms, such as "Luo Tianyi," who have amassed millions of fans. These virtual personas are computer-generated characters that interact with audiences in real-time, often using motion capture and voice synthesis technologies. The popularity of virtual anchors like Luo Tianyi blurs the boundaries between the virtual and the real, introducing new ethical challenges.

For instance, determining who is responsible for the words and actions of virtual anchors becomes complex. Is it the developers, the operators behind the scenes, or the AI algorithms themselves? Additionally, as users develop emotional attachments to these virtual figures, there are concerns about how these relationships affect social interactions and individual well-being. The emotional connections between users and virtual images raise questions about consent, manipulation, and the authenticity of experiences in virtual environments.

The mobility of human-machine ethics thus plays a critical role in shaping the future of the digital cultural industry, influencing how culture is produced, consumed, and experienced in the metaverse.

5 Discussion:New Approaches to the Development of the Digital Cultural Industry from the Perspective of Mobility

In the digital economy era, leveraging new productive forces to empower cultural innovation is a necessary path to promote the transformation, upgrading, and high-quality development of the digital cultural industry. The foundational technologies of the metaverse ("BIGANT," i.e., Blockchain, Interactivity, Gaming, Artificial Intelligence, Network and Computation, Internet of Things) are characterized by high technology, high efficiency, and high quality, aligning with the advanced productive force qualities of the new development concept, which improves the efficiency of cultural production resource allocation and creates new generations of cultural demand. In practical terms, metaverse technology still faces issues such as technological maturity, equipment costs, user experience, and content innovation in the construction of immersive and experiential cultural tourism integration. There is a path dependence on current technology iteration, industry development, and user habits (Xiang Yong, 2024). Currently, the cultural metaverse is still in its foundational stage but can already be applied to virtual large-scale gatherings, artistic creation, cultural relic protection, and other fields. The high-quality development of the digital cultural industry is China's development goal for the cultural industry. Emphasizing the construction of the cultural metaverse and continuously improving development quality is the appropriate choice for developing the digital cultural industry. The focus should be on the following aspects:

Firstly, establish a New Model for Cultivating Digital Nomads and Developing Virtual Clusters for the Digital Cultural Industry.

Enhance the digital literacy of digital nomads, ensuring they have a clear understanding and discernment of "metaverse + digital culture" and high production and creativity capabilities. Improve talent cultivation, evaluation, incentive, and mobility configuration mechanisms in the digital cultural industry, highlighting guidance management, innovative thinking, and practical training. Accelerate the cultivation of digital "cultural industry special envoys" covering rural, urban, aerospace, and deep-sea fields. At the same time, leverage the opportunity of "cloud computing and data empowerment" to achieve the goal of cultivating cross-regional cooperation clusters and standardize operational, management, and monitoring mechanisms.

Secondly, establish a Cultural Data Rights and Circulation System, and Develop Metaverse Digital Culture Legislation and Industry Standards.

For the complex systemic issues of the metaverse, China still faces urgent problems related to data security, cultural security, and copyright security. Emphasize the core position of data capital, complete data rights confirmation, data standardization and desensitization processing, data tabulation and evaluation, and data circulation platform construction.

Thirdly, establish identity identification, complete data ownership registration, and ensure smooth authorization mechanisms; standardize data cleaning and format requirements before transactions; assetize data, establish a data asset repository (including directory and service interfaces) after value assessment for easy retrieval and use; leverage the "data element×" multiplier effect to build a secure and trustworthy data trading platform, execute data trading agreements automatically through smart contracts, and complete data delivery and value transfer when preset conditions are met. At the same time, pre-research on fundamental universal standards for metaverse terminology, classification, identification, key technical standards for metaverse identity systems, content generation, cross-domain interoperability, and technology integration, service standards for virtual digital humans, digital asset flow, content rights confirmation, and asset protection, as well as privacy protection, content regulation, and data security standards, is particularly important.

Fourthly, formulate Guidance Policies for Digital Cultural Community Building and Cultivation of Digital Cultural Values.

Systematically and efficiently organize and coordinate efforts from government, universities, enterprises, society, and standardization agencies to develop policies for digital cultural communities and digital cultural values. Promote the construction of smart communities, improve network facilities within communities, and use digital technology to regularly hold various digital cultural and artistic theme activities in communities. Conduct offline digital cultural education activities to enhance the digital skills and digital ethics awareness of community residents.

6 Conclusion

In the context of globalization, China's digital cultural industry is aligning with the international digital cultural industry. It is foreseeable that, under the empowerment of metaverse technology, China's digital cultural industry will reduce costs and improve efficiency in all processes, including content planning, production, and marketing. Based on the review of domestic and foreign literature on "mobility," this paper explores the digital cultural industry from the perspective of the metaverse, focusing on the mobility of people and scenes in cultural space, cultural data and cultural memory, cultural concepts and aesthetics, and human-machine ethics, thereby refining theoretical constructs. The mobility of people and scenes in cultural space can be summarized as the shift from reality to virtuality, such as the transformation of cultural workers into digital nomads and the shift from cultural industry parks to virtual clusters. The mobility of cultural data and cultural memory is reflected in the data flow between virtual and real using technologies like VR, AR, and MR, relying on the cultural memory carried and inherited by "memory digital humans." The mobility of cultural concepts is embodied in the combination of "cyber culture + metaverse culture." The mobility of cultural aesthetics is both a visualization of the mobility of cultural concepts and a higher-level requirement for the digital cultural industry, necessitating attention to the transmission of Chinese imagery aesthetics and driving the upgrade of beauty through simulation, imitation, and creation. Finally, this paper proposes three new approaches for the development of the digital cultural industry: establishing a new model for cultivating digital nomads and developing virtual clusters; establishing a rights and circulation system for cultural data and developing metaverse digital culture legislation and industry standards; and formulating guidance policies for digital cultural community building and cultivation of digital cultural values. Only through multidimensional construction of comprehensive pathways for cultural data and cultural security can the coordination and symbiosis of the digital cultural industry and the cultural metaverse be achieved.

In the metaverse, socializing is no longer limited to entertainment but is evolving towards a new form of organization, developing into a community of identity, concepts, and values (Yu Jingdong, 2021). After the implementation of metaverse policies, there has been an explosion of industry participants. To achieve sustainable, high-quality, and stable development of the metaverse, digital cultural enterprises need to strengthen their technological research and development capabilities, systematically organize key technology R&D projects, actively participate in and lead the creation and updating of international technology standards, and local governments should actively promote cultural metaverse planning from a global perspective, focus on breaking through core technological bottlenecks in industry development, and efficiently coordinate multiple stakeholders to form a collaborative force. The "enterprise + government" model should drive China's international technology standard setting and leading R&D in the metaverse field.

The inclusiveness and openness demonstrated by the mobility paradigm break the existing constraints of cultural production, allowing individuals with different backgrounds and technological levels to freely express themselves. This brings richer and more diverse creativity to the cultural industry and enables interactive production and consumption by digital cultural producers represented by virtual artists, AI creators, and digital influencers. Similarly, future research needs to further explore the new qualities and superior qualities of the metaverse in relation to Chinese animation, games, aesthetics, generative art, and other cultural industries, nurturing industry vitality, promoting fairness and sustainability, and enhancing China's strategic advantage in the global digital cultural industry competition.

References

Baker, J., Nam, K., Dutt, C.S.: A user experience perspective on heritage tourism in the metaverse: empirical evidence and design dilemmas for VR. Inf. Technol. Tourism **25**(3), 265–306 (2023)

Buhalis, D., Leung, D., Lin, M.: Metaverse as a disruptive technology revolutionising tourism management and marketing. Tour. Manage. **97**, 104724 (2023)

Colombo, F.: Reviewing the cultural industry: from creative industries to digital platforms. Commun. Soc. **31**(4), 135–146 (2018)

Dwivedi, Y.K., et al.: Metaverse beyond the hype: Multidisciplinary perspectives on emerging challenges, opportunities, and agenda for research, practice and policy. Int. J. Inf. Manage. **66**, 102542 (2022)

Gursoy, D., Malodia, S., Dhir, A.: The metaverse in the hospitality and tourism industry: an overview of current trends and future research directions. J. Hosp. Market. Manag. **31**(5), 527–534 (2022)

Hwang, G.J., Chien, S.Y.: Definition, roles, and potential research issues of the metaverse in education: an artificial intelligence perspective. Comput. Edu. Artif. Intell. **3**, 100082 (2022)

Kye, B., et al.: Educational applications of metaverse: possibilities and limitations. J. Edu. Eval. Health Prof. **18** (2021)

Magaudda, P., Marco, S.: Platform studies and digital cultural industries. Sociologica **14**(3), 267–293 (2020)

Massi, M., Vecco, M., Lin, Y.: Digital Transformation in the Cultural and Creative Industries. Digital Trans. Cultural Creative Ind. 1–9 (2020)

Narin, N.G.: A content analysis of the metaverse articles. J. Metaverse **1**(1), 17–24 (2021)

Park, S.M., Kim, Y.G.: A metaverse: taxonomy, components, applications, and open challenges. IEEE Access **10**, 4209–4251 (2022)

Peukert, C.: The next wave of digital technological change and the cultural industries. J. Cult. Econ. **43**(2), 189–210 (2019)

Raimo, N., et al.: Digitalization in the cultural industry: evidence from Italian museums. Int. J. Entrep. Behav. Res. **28**(8), 1962–1974 (2022)

Wang, Y., et al.: A survey on metaverse: Fundamentals, security, and privacy. IEEE Commun. Surv. Tutorials **25**(1), 319–352 (2022)

Wang, H., et al.: A survey on the metaverse: the state-of-the-art, technologies, applications, and challenges. IEEE Int. Things J. **10**(16), 14671–14688 (2023)

Yang, S.: Storytelling and user experience in the cultural metaverse. Heliyon, **9**(4) (2023)

Buhalis, D., Karatay, N.: Mixed reality (MR) for generation Z in cultural heritage tourism towards metaverse. In: Proceedings of ENTER 2022 eTourism Conference, Springer International Publishing, pp. 16–27 (2022)

Adey, P.: Mobility. Routledge (2017)

Cresswell, T.: Towards a politics of mobility. Environ. Plann. D: Soc. Space **28**(1), 17–31 (2010)

Sorokin, P.A.: "Social and cultural mobility", in Social Stratification, Class, Race, and Gender in Sociological Perspective, pp. 303–308. Second Edition, Routledge (2019)

Author Index